UNSTUCK & UNSTOPPABLE

SHAKE OFF THE PAST,
FIND YOUR PURPOSE,
GET ON WITH YOUR LIFE.

JIMN KYLES

FOREWORD BY CHRIS HODGES

MARY WELLS (FND)

Published by Anchor Bend Publishing

anchor bend
PUBLISHING

ISBN (print): 978-1-951022-16-7
ISBN (ebook): 978-1-951022-17-4

Printed in the United States of America

Jimn's Thanks

First and foremost, Jesus, I belong to You, always and forever.

Phyllis, you're my life partner. I'll never stop pursuing your heart. Thank you for loving me and always going on this crazy life journey with me—I love you.

Caden, Carson, Addison, and Raylin, I love you always and forever. Thank you for sharing your daddy with the world. You are the joy of my life.

Mom, your unconditional love and support are the reason I am who I am. A special thanks to my dad, who is worshiping Jesus in heaven. You have always embodied the heart of God. I love you always.

Thank you to my pastor, Chris Hodges, for loving me and investing your life into me. I am a better husband, father, and pastor because of you.

Finally, I want to say thank you to my brother Steve. Not only are you my biggest cheerleader but also my best friend. Apart from God, you're the reason I finished this book. I often felt overwhelmed, and yet you would never let me quit. Instead, you kept pushing me, encouraging me, and lifting me.

Acknowledgments

My sincere gratitude goes to the following individuals who helped refine this project and bring the vision to life. Each of you believed in me and in the vision of helping people get unstuck and become all that God created them to be. You poured countless hours into this project. You're the best team ever.

Peter Johnston, Randy Powell, Robin Nealy Carter, Vanessa Hill, Adriana Durham and Rica Lim, thank you for your professional insight and perspective that added so much to this message.

Contents

Foreword

By Chris Hodges

One of the most significant challenges for followers of Jesus is to avoid getting stuck without realizing it. No matter how long we've been walking with the Lord, no matter how passionate our commitment to knowing Him, no matter how much time we spend serving and ministering to others, most of us eventually hit a wall. We try to keep going until we wake up one day and realize we don't know how to move forward. We grow weary of trying harder and feel uncertain about convictions we once held as absolute truth. We no longer feel confident in our ability to trust God with our uncertainty.

The obstacle blocking our path may be an unexpected loss, a devastating disappointment, or a bitter betrayal that shakes the foundation of our faith. These painful moments often cause us to question our understanding of God and reflect on whether what we believe about Him is true. Times like these can move us forward in our faith, or they can become like quicksand which causes us to sink into doubt, distrust, and disobedience, eventually leaving us stuck.

A crisis of faith is not always the result of an obvious event or identifiable loss. Sometimes as we grow in our relationship with God, we simply reach a plateau. We begin to feel distant and disconnected from Him. We no longer hear the voice of His Spirit the way we once did. We wonder why He hasn't lived up to our expectations and the timetable we imagined for our lives. We might begin looking elsewhere to find meaning and significance in our lives. Slowly and almost imperceptibly, this kind of spiritual erosion can also leave us paralyzed in our faith.

Regardless of the cause, getting unstuck requires a fresh perspective on who God is and what He says is true. Moving forward happens when we recognize false beliefs and wrong assumptions in our thinking and replace them with the powerful truth of God's Word. Gaining spiritual momentum relies on allowing the Holy Spirit to refuel the engine of our faith, not our circumstances or emotions.

Getting unstuck is rarely easy, which is why I'm so excited about what my friend and fellow pastor, Jimn Kyles, has written in the pages that follow.

I first met Jimn at an ARC (Association of Related Churches) training event. He and his wife had recently launched a new life-giving church, Anchor Bend, in Richmond, Texas and he was helping to train and equip future church planters to go out and do the same.

Everything appeared to be going great for Jimn— his marriage, family, and church were all thriving. And yet, he would later confide in me that something was missing. Jimn had experienced a profound loss that rocked his world. It shook his confidence, leaving him feeling afraid, insecure, and overwhelmed by all the demands for his attention and energy. Jimn knew he was stuck. He just didn't know how to get unstuck. He was called, but wounded.

Identifying with so many of Jimn's inner struggles and the challenges of vocational ministry, I agreed to mentor him, to be his pastor and spiritual shepherd, not realizing just what a privilege and blessing it would be. Over the years, I have watched Jimn shift his focus from performance-based success to grace-based relationships. He began to grow and flourish not only with external success, but with internal transformation. Witnessing his dynamic progress, I'm sure I learned as much from him as he may have learned from me. And now you can, too.

Jimn wrote this book to help others get unstuck and move forward again on their spiritual journeys.

With hard-won insight and profound wisdom, he shares key truths from God's Word that helped him develop a strategy and forge tools for getting unstuck. He experienced the impact that knowing your true identity and divine purpose can have in every area of your life. In the pages ahead, Jimn makes it clear that we don't have to work harder and rely on our own strength to get going again. In fact, the secret to getting unstuck is just the opposite—surrendering ourselves completely to God's plan for our life.

As Jimn explains, when we allow God's Spirit to empower us, we discover more of who God created us to be instead of striving in our limited abilities. We realize our purpose here on earth and learn how to live it out. We experience more of the abundant, joyful life Jesus said He came to bring us. As we get unstuck and move in the divine direction God has for us, we become unstoppable!

This powerful spiritual rhythm is what I've witnessed in Jimn's own life and ministry over the years. As a pastor, leader, husband, father, friend, and ministry partner, Jimn now moves at the speed of grace. He faces the same slumps, bumps, and detours as the rest of us, but has learned how to overcome the barriers that get in our way, both within and without. He relies on God's power to sustain him as he lives out his purpose to advance God's kingdom. His example reminds me of how God loves to work in our lives so that we can experience the joy of living on purpose.

Whether you've been a believer for most of your life or you're still considering what it means to be a Christ-follower, this book will help you get unstuck and find your way. This book is a field guide for the journey of faith we all travel. While each path is different, the principles of God's Word remain the same. You don't have to resign yourself to going through the motions. You don't have to allow the enemy to lead you away from doing what God created you uniquely to do. Instead, I pray that what you hold in your hand will open your heart to a fresh, life-giving encounter with God as His Spirit breathes new life into you, right where you are. I hope that you will discover a renewed and richer sense of your divine purpose. Don't remain stuck, my friend, when you can become unstoppable!

—Chris Hodges

Pastor, Church of the Highlands
Author of *What's Next?* and *Out of the Cave*

Introduction

Everyone feels stuck at some point—especially in these present times. Life is full of ups and downs and unexpected twists and turns, but it's not what happens to you that matters most; it's how you respond to those unexpected moments.

In this book, we're going to look at some common pitfalls that can cause you to get stuck, and then we'll explore practical steps to overcome those pitfalls so that you can build the kind of life you have always dreamed of—a life full of purpose and passion, with boldness, courage, and the power to move your life forward so you can become unstoppable! That may sound like a lofty or far-off goal, but trust me, it's closer than you think.

2020 and a Global Pandemic

The year 2020 was unlike any other. I remember the excitement we all felt in January as we launched into not only a new year, but also into a brand-new decade. Twenty-twenty was the kickoff to a decade of hope and promise—one that was to be filled with expectation for a bright, limitless future.

Well, things didn't go as planned. In March, the world was turned upside down, and our lives were forever changed. Things we took for granted were no longer available to us: things like going to the movies, shopping, going to church, and eating out at a restaurant with friends and family. All gone. America was put on lockdown, and new terms such as "social distancing" were introduced and seared into the American psyche. We were given physical isolation as the primary prescription for the preservation of the health and safety of ourselves and others, especially the most vulnerable, including the elderly and those with preexisting conditions.

What's okay for
vacation is not okay
for everyday life.

This marked a turning point in our society and in our nation's history. We were forced to change the way we experience every aspect of life. Our world suddenly switched to an online environment where we all had to learn how to navigate this new digital reality. We shifted from virtual classrooms for our children to online campuses for our churches, from Zoom meetings for work to online shopping for all of our groceries and household essentials. We were encouraged to live in physical and social isolation. Even jobs were categorized as essential or nonessential.

In the beginning, I thought this would all pass quickly. "Two weeks to slow the spread." We can do this. I thought it was all temporary and couldn't fathom that this would go on for as long as it has. So, I was caught off guard and simply unprepared for the toll it would take on my mind over the long haul. Unknowingly, I went into the pandemic with the wrong mentality. I let my guard down. Without really thinking about it, I approached this new reality like I would approach a vacation. That doesn't mean it was easy or even enjoyable. It wasn't. It was actually one of the hardest seasons of my life—as it was for most people. When I say a "vacation mentality," what I mean is that I approached this as though it were simply a break from my schedule for a couple of weeks.

On vacation, I relax my standards and daily disciplines. I forego the routine that has helped me stay on track to move forward with my goals. On vacation, I don't set my alarm to wake up at 5 a.m. I intentionally sleep in and let my body enjoy extra rest. I lounge around the house in pajamas and workout clothes, even though I don't actually work out. I don't shave. I watch movies. And since it's "vacation," I typically splurge on my favorite unhealthy foods without feeling bad about it because hey . . . it's vacation.

As much as I enjoy vacation and splurging on all these things, I understand that I can't live life this way day in and day out. All good things must come to an end. If I were to live habitually with a vacation mentality, my life would be a total mess. What's okay for vacation is not okay for everyday life.

Looking back over 2020, at that early stage of Covid, I realize that because I thought the circumstances were temporary, it was easy for me to have a relaxed vacation mentality, which is an undisciplined mindset. It's not that I thought everything would be easy. I knew that staying home and changing the way we function in our daily lives would take work; however, I didn't realize this new way of life would extend for the entire year and have a lasting impact on our society. I thought, like many others, we would go back to the old way of life. It was unfathomable that social distancing could be adopted long-term, whether at school, work, commerce, church, or even in relational connections and friendships. Just about every group activity we experienced outside of our immediate family was encouraged to be conducted through a screen.

I remember the first time I realized the impact social distancing was having in my own life. It was in September 2020. We had been navigating the pandemic for six months, and the local restrictions were finally loosening up. I needed to see the doctor and get some blood work done, so I booked an appointment. The day arrived for my visit, so I grabbed my "personal protective equipment" and went to the medical office. I had just checked in with the front desk and was sitting in the lobby waiting to be called, when out of nowhere, a man I had never met decided to sit down right beside me. The office was empty and there were open and available seats all around the room. Even though we were both wearing masks, I have to be candid; it bothered me. I am a pastor and a Christian, but my space felt invaded. I thought to myself, *Wh … what are you doing, man? You're too close. I know you have a mask, but I don't know you or why you are here, and I am uncomfortable with you being so close to me.*

When I realized what I was thinking, I was shocked. My own thoughts caught me off guard. Just a couple of months earlier, that thought would never have crossed my mind. I wouldn't have thought twice about someone sitting next to me. It was in that moment I had an epiphany. I realized that the messaging around Covid-19 had impacted my life more than I'd realized. My psyche had been changed. I had been slowly conditioned to live afraid, as if fear is normal. When did I become afraid to have someone sit next to me? We were in a doctor's office, but he had a mask. I had a mask. There was no reason for me to feel the way I felt except that my thoughts weren't in the right place.

My point is, everyone has been affected by this season in one way or another and likely in ways we are not even aware. Being unprepared caused many people, myself included, to get stuck. Whether we got stuck with ungodly thoughts, bad habits, old relationships, unresolved pain, isolation, fear, or anything else, the outcome was the same—life stalled and we could no longer see the hope of a bright future.

But may I share something with you? Your circumstances don't determine how bright your future is. You can start altering your life today. When I took inventory of my own mentality, I made some immediate and effective changes. What I discovered was that the same thing that was holding me back was holding many others back. As I shared my journey with friends and family, and through speaking engagements across the country, the feedback was overwhelming. This book is my journey of getting unstuck. Consider this a blueprint for your journey to get unstuck no matter what has happened in your past or in your present. I have made the decision, with my family's support, to be vulnerable and transparent with you in a way that's rare for public figures. But I knew that in order to help you transform, I needed to get real and raw.

A dear friend of mine once told me something I have never forgotten. It's a quote by Howard Hendricks: "You can impress from a distance, but you can only impact up close." This book is certainly not my attempt to impress anyone. More than anything, I want to impact your life in a profound way and help you see that no matter what is happening around you, you can live life to the fullest, the way God intended. You may have felt stuck. We've all been there, but you don't have to stay there. God is calling you to a place of freedom, strength, and empowerment—a place where you become unstoppable through Him.

Before we go on this journey together, I would like to mention one last thing. In this book, you will see that I use the word *paradigm*. Because paradigms are integral to helping us become unstuck and move toward being unstoppable, allow me to explain upfront where I am going. Addressing paradigm spirituality in his book, *Conformed to His Image*, author and speaker Ken Boa defines a paradigm as "a way of seeing based on implicit or explicit rules that shape one's perspective." He distinguishes between two primary paradigms—temporal and eternal. He adds, "We can live as if this world is all there is, or we can view our earthly existence as a brief pilgrimage designed to prepare us for eternity."

I have found that when I have gotten stuck, it has been because I have fallen into a temporal paradigm trap and missed the underlying truth of the eternal paradigm sometimes hidden below the surface to which I was somehow blinded. It is possible to live with a temporal paradigm in one area of our lives while living with an eternal paradigm in another.

Because truths regarding these two different perspectives and values are fundamental to our freedom, I will be periodically returning to this idea of paradigms as I relate some of my experiences and then get into the four foundational building blocks of life.

CHAPTER 1

Help, I'm Stuck!

While it's true that you might be stuck,
with God you are never stranded.

"When you get there, you gotta gun it."

My wife, Phyllis, was a bit perplexed by her sister-in-law's last statement before she lost cell signal and dropped the call. *Was this some sort of riddle? Get where? Gun what?* Phyllis tried to call Stephanie back, but the call would not go through. It was a Saturday morning, and they were meeting up in Matagorda, a well-known Texas hotspot for fishing and beach activities about an hour and a half from where we live. They had planned a day of adventure with the kids, and because of other obligations, they drove separately and planned to meet up once they got there.

Stephanie would arrive just before Phyllis and agreed to send a pin drop of her exact location on the beach. Prior to that, the two had been in constant communication all morning, going over the details of the day and making sure they had all the beach-going accoutrements. The kids were buzzing with excitement, and everyone was looking forward to a day of fun in the sun. Phyllis fully expected to be able to call Stephanie when she was getting close, but now she couldn't get a hold of her.

Phyllis wasn't too worried since she had the location pin; however, it never dawned on her that she might lose cell service when she got close. My wife is a beautiful, carefree, easy-going kind of person. She has a very keen sense of direction and is very capable of managing a lot of details. She puts up with me and our four kids, so she knows how to get it done! But that day she found herself in an unfamiliar area, with no working phone, and no other help to get to the place she was supposed to meet up with Stephanie. All she knew was that she was getting close and was running into Saturday beach traffic. She figured if she could just get onto the beach, she could drive on the sand until she saw Stephanie's car. After all, she had a general idea of where she was.

Phyllis was slowly driving along the main drag, looking for a beach access road. She finally saw a clearing in the brush and a sign that said, "Nature Trail Access," so she figured that must be the way to get to the beach and nature trails. She turned on to this apparent access road and, to her surprise, she didn't see any cars. Thankful to be out of traffic, she exclaimed, "Well, praise God! I've got the whole beach to myself." She was certain that in no time she'd run into Stephanie. What she didn't realize is that nobody was there because the road she was on wasn't a road at all—it was a washed-up trail for people to walk on, not intended for cars. Completely unaware of this important fact, Phyllis continued down the sand-filled trail and came to an impasse in the road. There was a deep sandy ravine in front of her, and in any other circumstance, she would never consider trying to cross it, but in that moment she remembered her sister-in-law's final words of wisdom: "When you get there, you gotta gun it."

Phyllis paused for a second. The common-sense angel on one shoulder whispered "turn around" in one ear, while Stephanie's admonition to "gun it" rang loudly in the other. Like any other God-fearing mother headed to the beach with her children, Phyllis took her foot off the brake and gunned it! Lo and behold, sand started flying everywhere as her tires spun and thrust the vehicle forward. She ran headlong into the embankment, sending the nose of our SUV into the air, and then she suddenly stopped. When the sand settled, she realized she had high-centered our SUV and was stuck. Not just a little stuck; she was for real stuck! She shifted to reverse and hit the gas again, trying desperately to undo what she'd just done. The more she tried to get unstuck, the deeper her tires sank into the sand.

In complete panic, she jumped out of the car, got the kids out, and had the brilliant idea to grab the beach toys they'd packed earlier and have the kids help her dig the sand out from underneath the vehicle. They worked for forty-five minutes with plastic shovels and buckets, doing everything possible to get unstuck, to no avail. Our son Carson was twelve at the time and the only one tall enough to reach the pedals, so at one point Phyllis had him jump in the driver's seat while she tried to push the vehicle out! She was desperate and had tried everything. Finally, realizing the only way to get out of this situation was to find help, she began to walk down the beach. She spotted a truck off in the distance and flagged the driver down. He thankfully had a chain and tools to pull them out and help them get unstuck.

How often in life do we get stuck because we become disconnected—from God, family, friends, church, and community? When I have become stuck in my life, it always traces back to my getting disconnected from God. Somewhere along the way, I got busy or distracted. I would be doing good when all of a sudden the connection with God was lost, but instead of quickly reconnecting with Him, I just kept going. I didn't stop because I was busy with life and thought I could figure it out on my own, but it didn't take long before I would take a wrong turn and end up stuck. Proverbs 14:12 says, "There is a path before each person that seems right, but it ends in death." Without God, it's easy to think you're going the right way, just like Phyllis, even when it's the wrong way.

While it's true that we all get stuck at times, that doesn't mean you're stranded. To be stuck is to be held back, to be detained by circumstances. For example, "My car broke down, so I'm stuck until my wife picks me up." But that doesn't mean I'm stranded. I have a way home. I have options. Being stranded is different from being stuck. Stranded means you have no options or no way around your current circumstance. To be stranded is to be without hope.

Some of you have been stuck so long that you think you're stranded. We have a real enemy, the devil, whose mission is to steal, and to kill, and to destroy (John 10:10). Your enemy has been speaking into your mind saying, "Your marriage will never…" "Your kids will never…" "Your finances will never…" "Your health will never…" I'm sure you can fill in the blanks. You started by feeling stuck, and then those feelings festered until now you feel stranded. You feel like your current situation is hopeless. You know God is real; you know He loves you. You know you are saved and going to heaven, but you've given up all hope in this one area, or maybe in multiple areas of life. You see the situation as hopeless because you are seeing through your feelings. Maybe you're reading this, and you don't have hope because you've never had hope. You don't know God. You've never had a relationship with Him. If that's you and you want to change that, it's as simple as praying this prayer:

If you prayed that prayer, send me an email at mystory@ jimnkyles.com

I want to hear what God has done in your life.

God in heaven, here I am. Right now, I'm ready to surrender everything to You. I can't do this life on my own and I don't want to try anymore. I'm ready right now to go all in. Have Your way in me. Show me Your love, show me grace, show me Your power so I can experience Your salvation and fulfill Your purpose for my life. In Jesus' name, amen.

But no matter where you are coming from, where you are headed, or what you are presently going through—no matter how hopeless your situation might seem, as long as you are breathing—there is hope! God can take the worst situation, turn it around, and bring good out of it. He is working on your behalf. Even if you can't see it or feel it, hold on because a breakthrough is coming! I want to encourage you with the words of the apostle Paul in Philippians 1:6, "I am certain that God, who began the good work within you, will continue his work until it is finally finished on the day when Christ Jesus returns" (NLT). Let this truth sink down into your spirit: As long as you're breathing, God's not done with you!

How Do I Get Unstuck?

One day I was sitting in my bedroom spending time with God. That day I felt stuck over a personal issue, and I was having a little pity party for myself. Yes, this pastor had a pity party. I have problems, struggles, and challenges just like everybody else. That day, instead of crying out to God, I was just crying to God. I was asking God, "How do I get unstuck?"

When I was finished, I opened my *One Year Bible* reading assignment for the day: Acts 28. I had just read Acts 27 the day before about the apostle Paul being shipwrecked, and I couldn't stop thinking about it all day. I was eager to dive into the rest of the story, and the timing couldn't have been better.

I began reading Acts 28 and my jaw dropped when I got to verse ten: "... and when we were ready to sail, they furnished us with the supplies we needed." It was like something exploded in my spirit! I had previously read this story more times than I can count, and I have never noticed what I saw that day, "And when they were ready…" See, three months had passed since Paul had first been shipwrecked on the island. We don't know everything that happened during that time, but we do know that the Bible says, "when we were ready." Paul was a prisoner at the time, so it's not like he could just get up and leave when he wanted to. The Roman guards would have made the decision for Paul, but we know that they couldn't do anything without God allowing it to happen. It is safe to say that God opened the door for Paul to leave the island when His work there had been fulfilled. Paul was stuck, but he wasn't stranded.

As I read this, I sat there thinking, "*Okay, God. I know You are talking to me.*" Those four words, *when they were ready*, just marinated in my spirit. *When they were ready*, God provided a way out for them. Paul redeemed the time while he was there and made the most out of a bad situation. Then, after fulfilling his assignment, God supplied everything he needed through the people to move on.

Waiting on God is not passive. It doesn't mean you sit by and do nothing. No, when you are passive, you can easily become a victim, meaning you let life happen to you. Instead, you are to be an active partner with God and prepare yourself to be ready. John Maxwell is credited with saying, "Most people want to change the world to improve their lives, but the world they need to change first is the one inside themselves." Don't wait for someone or something else to change or to help you change or make your situation better. Change doesn't start from the outside; it starts from within.

Here's what I felt the Lord said to my heart that day: "When you're ready, Jimn, I'll provide a way for you to move your life and the church forward." It was a strong word, and I loved it! God reaffirmed to me that being stuck and waiting for God to help me was no time for passivity. I had a part to play if I wanted to see my life change. I was the only person who could, with God's help, bring change, and I am the only one who can hold change up. I am the only one who can limit what God does in my own life, and you are the only one who can limit what God does in your life. It doesn't matter who likes you or dislikes you or unfriends you on social media. It doesn't matter what people say about you, or even what they say *to* you. Paul was initially received on the island with kindness, but then he was abruptly thought to be a murderer. Regardless of the change in attitude of the islanders toward him, Paul pressed on, eventually healing many on the island. Subsequently, those who had been judgmental toward Paul became vehicles for provision for him and others as they readied to depart from the island. In the same way, don't be surprised if God uses the very people who were critical or judgmental toward you to provide what you need to move into your next season of life!

But also notice that Paul refused to be a victim. He wasn't going to wait and see what was going to happen in his life. He chose to respond and not react to his tough situations, and God was able to move in a powerful way through him to bring healing and hope to the island of Malta. For the three months following their landing at Malta, God performed great miracles through the hands of Paul. God used a bad situation, a situation that would cause many people to become angry and frustrated, to bring hope and healing to the entire island.

Know this: God never wastes your pain. He wants to take your pain and make it a source of great impact. That's why Satan, the devil, works so hard to keep you distracted. Satan will do everything in his power to keep you focused on your circumstances . . . on what you don't have . . . on the people who don't like you or who disagree with you. Where focus goes, life flows, and when you concentrate your focus on people and circumstances that hold you back, you certainly won't see the potential of what God wants to do in and through your situation to reach people with a message of hope and healing.

No More Excuses

So how do you get ready? Getting ready starts by taking responsibility. But here's the challenge: It's always easier to make excuses than it is to take responsibility. Anyone can make an excuse for why they are stuck. We feel better about ourselves when we can shift the focus onto someone or something else. Have you ever said or thought anything like the following:

- My marriage is hopeless because my spouse won't change.
- I'm stuck financially. I can't get a better job ... don't have a car ... don't have a college degree.
- I'm not qualified. I didn't go to college ... didn't graduate high school ... don't have a GED.
- I can't serve in my church. I don't have time. I wouldn't even know what to do.
- I can't go to small group. I don't know anybody. I'm too busy.

- I can't be generous. I'm barely making ends meet. I can't afford it.

While any or all of these may be true, they are all excuses. Excuses can hold you back for the rest of your life, but they don't have to. Two people can be in the same situation, and one is a victim while the other uses that challenge to do something great for God. One says, "I can't," and one says, "I can." One says, "It won't work," and one says, "It will." So you have to make a decision. Are you going to keep making excuses or start taking responsibility? When you take responsibility, you are showing God that you're ready, often a catalyst for Him to make His next move.

It takes courage to take responsibility. It really does. If I blame you, and I blame the church, and I blame God, and I blame my boss, and I blame my upbringing, and I blame my past, and I blame my last name, and I blame my bank account, then I never have to take responsibility. I never have to change. I can stay tucked away in my comfort zone and remain ineffective all day long by placing the blame on others.

But the day I take responsibility, change my temporal perspective to an eternal perspective, stop blaming people, and step out and step up, that's the day I allow the courage of God to rise up within me.

I allow His power to flow through me, and I open the door for His provision to come to me. We have to realize that we have arrived where we are today because of our past choices. And if things happened in my life that weren't my choice, it doesn't matter because God will raise me up out of that situation.

As a Christian, you have Christ living inside of you. 1 John 4:4 says, "The one who is in you is greater than the one who is in the world." The Jesus inside of you is greater than any opposition you might be facing today. The question is, will you allow Christ to be your champion to help you be free? Will you have the courage to say yes and take responsibility? It takes courage to take a chance; it takes courage to take a risk. You can't be worried about what people think about you because that fear will hold you back. So, here's the question you have to ask yourself: "Am I trying to build my reputation or God's?"

My answer is simple: God's.

When you realize that whatever God speaks, God will do, it takes the pressure off you. You are responsible for obedience; God is responsible for the outcome. You have to be willing to be courageous.

Now, let me warn you about something. You need to understand that once you make the choice to take responsibility to be courageous, sometimes your life will take an unexpected route.

One time I was preparing to fly from Dallas to California for a seminar where I was speaking later that evening. I made plans to leave early in the morning to make sure and catch my flight. But the next morning I was running late, ran into unexpected traffic, and got held up in the security lines. By the time I got to the gate, I had missed my flight. I was desperate, frustrated, and stressed, but I still needed to get to California that night, so I went to the ticket counter and pleaded for assistance. The customer service agent told me, "I can get you there today, but there are no direct flights." At that point,

> You are responsible
> for obedience;
> God is responsible
> for the outcome.

I didn't care. I said, "I'll take whatever you've got." So she booked me on a new flight—one that made a stop in Atlanta before going to California. I had to go in the opposite direction of where I wanted to end up before I could get on the correct route to my final destination.

God also has a way of redirecting our lives. Sometimes we are off course by our own doing: I missed the flight. Sometimes it's not our own doing: flights get redirected. Either way, sometimes you can't move forward from where you are.

- Maybe you get laid off at work. Perhaps it's time to develop that business idea you've been dreaming about. (Besides, you didn't like your job anyway.)

- Schools are closed and you're forced to homeschool your kids—an unexpected answer to your prayers that God would help you better connect with them.

- You're suddenly working from home and discovering a surprising improvement in your work/life balance.

- Churches in rented facilities, forced to close, are discovering they can reach even more lost people than before through online technology.

I know it often feels awkward and backward when God is redirecting us. Yet we must trust Him to realign our lives with His plan. I'm not saying God caused your situation, but I am saying that He will use it to get you into position. T.D. Jakes says it like this,

"Your setback is a set up for a comeback." God can use your situation, no matter how bad it is, to get you in position for where He is taking you. The farther back you pull the rubber band on a slingshot, the more tension is created, and the farther the projectile will go when you release it. It's the same with us. You may experience the tension, the pain, and the stretching, yet feel like you aren't getting anywhere. But get ready! It might be a divine setup to launch you farther ahead. Don't let discouragement or disappointment cause you to miss what God wants to do in your life.

If you're at the end of your rope and ready to quit, don't do it! Let me help you. Know that I've been on the journey you are taking. Let this book be your tour guide. This is your season to move forward with God's help. He wants to lead you into a place of self-discovery and growth, a place where you can experience God's freedom from whatever has held you back. If you're ready, let's begin.

Scan here to listen to my podcast, **"Unstuck and Unstoppable."** *It is my desire that this podcast would be a resource to you, and help you get unstuck and become unstoppable in your life.*

CHAPTER 2

When Life Bites You

*God can take your place of pain and
make it a place of impact.*

We've all been bitten by life. I don't even have to go into detail because I'm sure you know exactly what I'm talking about. But when something bad happens, we have a choice to make.

As discussed in Chapter One, the apostle Paul recounted a series of hardships that came his way in Acts chapters 27 and 28. Maybe you can relate. First, he was a prisoner traveling to Rome to stand trial before Caesar. Then, along the way he found himself in the middle of a storm. He warned those in charge not to continue because he anticipated that something bad was going to happen. Yet, they didn't listen to him and he was forced to continue the journey against his will and better judgment. Ultimately, they were shipwrecked and ended up on the island of Malta.

Paul gathered a pile of brushwood for a fire. As he put the wood on the fire, a viper crawled out, bit him, and latched on to his hand. After all that had happened,

Paul was standing there with a poisonous snake dangling from his hand. When the local islanders saw what had happened, they said to each other, "This man must be a murderer!" Talk about being kicked when you're down. It wasn't bad enough that he was stranded and shipwrecked. Not bad enough he got bitten by a snake. Now they were telling him *why* he got bitten! They said he must be a murderer who, even though he had escaped from the sea, would not be allowed to live by the goddess Justice. But to everyone's surprise, "Paul, shook the snake off into the fire . . ." And my favorite part, ". . . and suffered no ill effects" (Acts 28:5).

Now think for a moment about how you would have responded in this situation. Our choice during difficulty is this: We can either focus on the lies of the world and let that situation drain us, derail us, or make us angry, frustrated, bitter, and stuck; or we can choose to believe God. Romans 8:28 says, "And we know that God causes everything to work together for the good of those who love God and are called according to His purpose for them" (NLT). That's a powerful promise!

Think about what could have happened if Paul had gotten offended and frustrated and angry like so many of us would have today. What if he had said,

"Look, don't you know who I am? I am the Apostle Paul. I'm God's chosen to preach to you Gentiles and I have written divinely inspired letters to multiple churches even revealing previously hidden truths."

See, it's human nature to address the critics and defend ourselves. But really, all that does is get us stuck in our circumstances. Instead, we need to do what Paul did and just shut our mouths and shake it off!

Let me remind you again about what happened after Paul shook the snake off into the fire. Scripture says, "He suffered no ill effects." I love this because even though the devil attacks, it doesn't mean he'll win. Even though he lashes out at you, it doesn't mean he can harm you. You don't have to agree with what the enemy is trying to do in your life. Just because the enemy has attacked your business, you don't have to buy into the lie and think, "Now I'm going to lose my business." No, stand in faith. Don't "add your faith" to the report of the enemy. Instead, believe the report of the Lord and what His Word says about you.

Paul suffered no ill effects, and even though the people expected him to swell up and suddenly fall dead, he didn't. In fact, nothing happened to him at all. After watching this and seeing nothing bad happen to him, they changed their minds and said he was not a criminal. In fact, they went to the opposite end of the spectrum and started calling him a god. What the enemy meant for evil for Paul, God turned around for his good. God used this situation to give Paul credibility in the eyes of the leaders of the island.

Paul had great favor with one of the leaders on the island, Publius. Scripture says, "[Publius] welcomed us to his home and showed us generous hospitality for three days" (Acts 28:7). While there, Paul discovered that Publius's father was sick in bed, suffering from fever and dysentery. Paul prayed for him and the healing power of God restored him. Just like that! Paul ended up in a place where he would have never been otherwise.

Then something really amazing happened. Others who were sick in Malta came to Paul, and he prayed for them and they were cured. God turned Paul's situation around. The devil thought he had him, but it was actually a divine setup for revival. God took those painful moments in Paul's life and used them to bring hope and healing to the entire island. Even though Paul was a prisoner, even though he was in a violent storm and eventually shipwrecked, even though Paul was bitten by a venomous snake, it all eventually turned out to give him credibility with the people of the island. They assumed he must be a god.

WHEN LIFE BITES YOU

We know that Paul wasn't a god, but he was standing, he was speaking, he was living on behalf of the one true living God, and because of that, he responded the right way in the midst of adversity, and he had influence with the leader of the island. Because Paul shook off all the adversities that had come his way, revival came to an island. What was meant to kill him, what was meant to destroy him, actually set him up to have great kingdom impact!

Paul had to make the same choice I'm asking you to make. It's easy to react improperly when bad things happen. Paul could have pouted and refused to do anything for the people because they said mean and hurtful things about him when they didn't even know him. He could have cursed them and become defensive when they said he must be a murderer. He could have refused to go spend time with the leader of the island. He could have overlooked his opportunity to pray for Publius's dad. He could have refused to pray for the sick and hurting. Paul could have reacted to the pain he was experiencing and would have been fully justified in the eyes of his peers. No one would have blamed him. In fact, most people would have affirmed Paul and told him he was fully justified. However, Paul knew better. He chose to respond and not react. He didn't let his emotions cause him to say or do anything negative. Even in the midst of pain, Paul chose kindness and love. He refused to be offended and instead forgave all those who hurt him. It's his response that allowed God to take his pain and give it purpose.

We see that bad things happened in Paul's life, yet he was not a victim. He was not bitter, he was not angry, he was not offended or frustrated. He chose a different response and his life made an eternal impact.

Maybe you're under a lot of pressure like Paul was, and you are trying to release the pressure by talking about it. However, you can disqualify yourself just by talking. Notice that Paul didn't say a word; he just lived it out. Sometimes you just have to live it out. Often, when you feel the pressure building up around you, it's because God is doing something within you.

God is all powerful! He is so great! Obedience to God will put you in places you could never put yourself. God wants to take your pain and give it purpose.

It's like when Phyllis cooks a roast in the Crock-Pot on a Sunday morning. She gets up early, puts the roast in with some spices, adds some water, and then puts the lid back on and turns the heat up. Without the heat and steam, the meat, spices, and water would simply sit there and eventually spoil. One thing I have learned after twenty-two years of marriage is that no matter what, you don't take the lid off or you're in trouble! I used to walk by frequently, pick the lid up, and check on the meat to see how it was coming along. One time Phyllis caught me and started fussing. She said, "No wonder it's taking so long! Every time you lift the lid you extend the time it takes to cook the roast." I didn't realize it at the time, but when I lifted the lid, I let out the heat and pressure needed to cook the roast to perfection.

Similarly, God uses all of the pressures of life, the hard times and tough situations we experience, to perfect us. He works out His character and nature within us. That's why James says, "Consider it pure joy, my brothers and sisters, whenever you face trials of many kinds, because you know that the testing of your faith produces perseverance. Let perseverance finish its work so that you may be mature and complete, not lacking anything" (James 1:2-4).

Every time you react in a tough situation by saying something negative, or becoming defensive, or responding with spite or malice, it releases the pressure from our lives that God is using to perfect us. I am not saying that God causes the hard situations.

I just want you to know that He will ultimately use them to work out His purpose in your life.

Maybe your spouse cheated on you. That wasn't God's plan. It's incredibly painful to experience that kind of betrayal. But you still have a choice. Maybe your business failed even though you submitted it to God; you did everything you thought was right and somehow it still shut down. Maybe your kids are off course, or a loved one died. Something bad has happened in your life and it doesn't seem fair. But what we see with Paul is that God took his pain and turned it into purpose, but only after Paul surrendered the pain that he experienced. He allowed God to do what He wanted to do through that difficulty, and God turned it all around.

God Can Only Redeem
What You're Willing to Surrender

When we experience pain, oftentimes the hardest thing to do is to surrender that pain to God. We want to hold on to it because as bad as it is to experience, the pain allows us to feel justified in the way we behave and treat those who hurt us. Maybe a friend betrayed you or a leader used you. Maybe a loved one said or did something that devastated you. They hurt you, and

WHEN LIFE BITES YOU

so in your mind, retribution is justified. It feels good to hold on to the pain and say, "You did me wrong and now I am going to pay you back." The problem is, that's the opposite of what the Bible says for us to do. The Bible says, "Love your enemies and pray for those who persecute you" (Matthew 5:44). Wow, that can be a hard thing to do, but if we want God to redeem the pain and to use it for His glory, we have to learn to release it and let it go.

How Do We Let It Go?

The Bible tells us to do good to those who do evil to us. I have found that many times the ones that hurt us the most don't even realize the pain and trauma they have caused. They may not even realize the enemy used them to wound our hearts deeply. The best thing we can learn to do is to follow Paul's example.

My youngest daughter, Raylin, sings it all the time, "Let it Go! Let it Go!" It's her favorite song from the movie, *Frozen*. Even though the movie was written to entertain little children, it has such deep spiritual truth. If only we could learn to let it go. But what does that mean? How do you *let it go*? You can try all day long to just ignore hurt and pain, which is what so many people try to do. They stuff it down, or drink it down, or just carry anger and bitterness and they don't even know why. But God has given us a powerful tool that we need to use every single day. There's one way and one way only to "let it go," and that is through forgiveness. I've heard it said this way: "Forgiveness is setting the prisoner free, and realizing the prisoner was you."[1] Forgiveness is a tool for you to be set free.

To forgive means to make a conscious, deliberate decision to release feelings of resentment or vengeance toward a person or group of people who have hurt or harmed you, regardless of whether or not they asked for it or "deserve" it in your estimation. Forgiveness is not defined by the effect on the other person, which is out of your control, but your choice to forgive does impact your open relationship with God (Matthew 6:14). Forgiveness does not mean forgetting, nor does it mean condoning or excusing what happened. You might say, "Look, they don't deserve my forgiveness. If you only knew..." I understand you may be hurting, but forgiveness is not about giving them what they deserve. It's about allowing you to move forward in your life. Forgiveness is for you to reflect the character of Christ and thereby receive the freedom of so doing regardless of the impact on the other person, which you cannot control. Forgiveness may have a positive impact of reconciliation, but it may not; nonetheless it is definitely designed to bring freedom to you as the original victim.

People get stuck in life because they won't surrender their pain to God. They refuse to forgive and allow God to heal their wounded heart. Forgiveness doesn't make what happened right; forgiveness makes *you* right.

Don't Drink the Poison

You have to understand that harboring unforgiveness is destructive to your soul. Unforgiveness includes engaging in ruminative thoughts of anger, vengeance, hate, and resentment, and it's toxic. It's like drinking poison and expecting the other person to die. The other person has most likely moved on. They've gone their way, yet you remain stuck and full of pain on the inside, poisoning yourself, thinking you are getting retribution by holding on to it, but really, it's killing you. Perhaps literally.

According to research by Dr. Michael Barry, sixty-one percent of all cancer patients have severe forgiveness issues. "When you harbor negative emotions,

> People get stuck in life
> because they won't
> surrender their pain to God.

anger and hatred create a state of chronic anxiety and chronic anxiety produces excess adrenaline and cortisol, which deplete the production of natural killer cells, which is your body's foot soldier in the fight against cancer."[2]

Unforgiveness increases anxiety and depression, elevates your blood pressure and vascular resistance, decreases your immune response, and worsens the effects of coronary artery disease. Don't drink the poison of unforgiveness. Choose to forgive just as Jesus teaches us to do in Matthew 18:21-22. Let it go!

You might say, "God, I want You to do it," and that's a good first step, but then you have to submit to His process. Be willing to give up your right to be right, your right to be heard, your right for revenge. Surrender it all to Him. If you'll give Him the pain, if you'll give Him that moment, if you'll give Him what's on the inside of your heart and say, "God, I release it all to You," I promise you, God can take that pain and turn it into purpose. God can do something supernatural because what's happening *in* you is more important than what happened *to* you. We have to ask, "God, what's in me? Is it offense, anger, bitterness?" It doesn't matter who didn't believe in you, who didn't give you a chance, or what your upbringing was. It's not about where you came from; it's about how you see yourself and where your trust is. Do you see yourself as a victim of your circumstances? Victims look at the external. Champions look at the internal.

A champion's mentality says, "I don't care what I have or what I don't have; I know that God has me in the palm of His hand. Because He has me, greater is He who is in me than he who is in this world." You have a promise in Isaiah 54:17 that no weapon formed against you shall prevail. That "snakebite" doesn't have to harm you.

No matter what the devil throws your way, remember God can use it as it's just a setup for a comeback! The greater the pain, the greater the promise. The greater the infliction, the greater the impact. I've seen it time and time again, and you will, too, if you choose to shake it off and surrender all to Him.

Moving Forward

I saw a meme online that said, "I'm getting tired of living through unprecedented events." Do you feel that way sometimes? Does it seem that every time we turn around, something unprecedented is happening? You might even be thinking, "Man, I feel like I'm going backward." I know I've felt that way at times. In the middle of 2020, there was a moment where I was questioning God: "God, are You going to do what You put in my heart? Are You going to keep Your word? Did I miss it somewhere?" But then I felt a strong response in my spirit: "Sometimes I have to take you backward to go forward."

Think about it. In 2020, we had state- and federally-mandated orders encouraging us to avoid people and crowds. It felt like we were moving backward in society. But in the middle of it all, did you find yourself getting closer to your family? Closer to your spouse and loved ones? My prayer has been to grow in my relationships and not become stagnant. I prayed to have a stronger marriage and a closer family. When the world shuts down and all you have is your family, it's the ideal opportunity to get closer to them! So, my prayer was answered, even though it felt like I had to go backward to go forward.

Not many parents woke up January 1, 2020, and said to themselves, *Gee, I think I would like to start homeschooling during the new year.* Yet lots of them had to rethink their plans and arrange for homeschooling.

Even so, I've heard many of them admit, "I didn't want to do this, but one thing that's happened is that I've gotten closer to my kids through this!" Some people lost their jobs and it felt like a setback. Yet at the same time, I've heard many stories of people who stepped out in a new direction and started a business they'd been dreaming about for years. Now they are living in a dream that they thought was dead, but God resurrected it for this moment.

Even when it looks like you're going backward, know that God has a plan. I was thinking about this as it relates to our church. During the early stages of the pandemic in March 2020, we had to go online because we hadn't purchased our campus yet. Without warning, the facility we were renting no longer allowed us to meet there. One Sunday I said, "I'll see you next week!" only to discover we had four days to become an internet church! It's tempting to think, *God, how is that moving forward?* I'll tell you this: Over the next twelve weeks, we reached more people than we ever had in the history of this church. Only God can do that! We were moving forward even though it didn't look the way we thought it would.

On a broader scale, on March 19, 2020, a prayer movement called Unite 714 was birthed when twenty-five pastors gathered to pray in response to the Covid-19 crisis. What started with a few pastors on a simple phone call exploded into a global prayer movement where millions of people in over 180 countries around the world began praying twice a day with one voice. As I write this, the movement is estimated to have impacted over one billion people around the world.[3]

Never in history have so many believers been unified, praying together for the same thing at the same time. No wonder the devil is mad! No wonder things are coming against our society, trying to divide us like never before. Why? Because the devil knows a church united cannot be defeated, and God is working to unite His church around the world.

In such uncertain times, be careful that you don't lose the joy of today because of the uncertainty of tomorrow. I love what the Psalmist said, "My future is in your hands" (Psalm 31:15 NLT). What does that mean? That means the future of our lives is in God's hands. Even though there is uncertainty, even though I may not know what tomorrow holds, I know the God who holds tomorrow and I know that He's got my life in His hands. Life may seem tough. It may look like a challenge and feel very difficult and confusing, but if we stay focused on Him, He will move our lives forward with Him.

When we are truly focused on Him, it doesn't matter what things look like. We're moving forward. When we are truly focused on Him, it doesn't matter what things feel like. We're moving forward. When we are truly focused on Him, it doesn't matter what's happening around us. We're moving forward. The only way we could ever lose is if we allow the devil to cause us to quit—because ultimately, the devil doesn't win. We may be in a struggle, we may experience pain that's hard, but the devil doesn't win. The only thing he can do is cause us to settle in a place where God intended for us to pass through. So let's make a quality decision that we are not going to settle. We're not going to stay stuck. We're not going to get stranded. We're not going to get left behind from what God wants to do.

Scan for your FREE **Help, I'm Stuck!** *ebook.*

CHAPTER 3

Don't Settle Where You Are

Never settle in a place God intended
for you to pass through.

One time, we planned a family vacation at Galveston Beach. As you may have noticed by now, we love the water. On this particular trip, Phyllis and I were going to leave two days early and have some "us" time alone as a couple. (When you take your kids with you, it's not really a vacation. It's more like a second job in a nicer location.) So we loaded up the truck and trailer and got everything ready for the beach. We had rented a beautiful waterfront cabin about two hours away. We weren't in a hurry. We thought, *We can check in at 4:30 p.m. and go have dinner. It's all going to be great. It's going to be amazing.*

We took off at 2:30 P.M. and headed down the highway, passing through Houston toward the beach. All of a sudden, one of the trailer tires blew. I really tried to remain calm because we didn't want to let anything get in the way of our vacation time. I pulled over and opened the back of the truck to find the jack to change the tire. But it was so packed we had to unload it on the side of an eight-lane highway! I could just feel the stares from the riders driving by. Well, after digging and searching and unpacking for thirty or forty minutes, I realized someone had "borrowed" my jack, so I couldn't even change the tire on the trailer if I wanted to!

So now we had to call roadside assistance. As you probably know, they're just not real "speedy." We waited another hour and a half. I kept saying under my breath, "Devil, you aren't stealing my joy." We tried to make the most of the time by finding some humor in it all. Finally, roadside assistance arrived and got the tire changed. We remained optimistic, thinking we could still get to Galveston at a decent time.

We started down the highway again. Thankfully there wasn't much traffic. We got about ten more miles down the road and you won't believe what happened—the tire on the other side of the trailer blew! Not like a "fix-a-flat" blowout, but more like "the-devil's-mad-and-pulled-a-pistol" kind of blowout. So now we were back on the side of the highway. No spare. No jack. Nothing for roadside assistance to work with if we called them.

We were thinking, *What in the world are we going to do?* I turned to Phyllis and suggested, "We can leave the trailer here. We have the blown tire in the back. Can we find a tire shop?" Well, it happened to be Memorial Day, and by now it was around 6:00 p.m., so all the major tire shops were closed. We kept calling around and finally reached someone at a "mom and pop" shop about five miles away. The kid on the phone said, "Well, it looks like we have one tire your size. That will be forty dollars." That sounded like a deal to me! With no other options, we disconnected the trailer, jumped in the truck, and headed off to find the replacement. Yes, it was a little risky, but I figured if somebody could actually steal the trailer without a tire, they could have it!

We got to the tire shop right before they closed. We paid for the tire, loaded it in the truck, and called the Toll Road Authority to help us because we still didn't have a jack. They agreed to send someone out to meet us at the trailer. Thankfully, the trailer was right where we left it. We put the new tire on the trailer, and I kid you not—we found a gash so deep on the inside wall that the wires were showing through. We had been in such a hurry that we didn't see it at the shop. There was a reason that tire was only forty dollars. I told the man from roadside assistance, "You might as well just put it on there because at least it's a tire that's aired up."

So there we were. I said, "Well, Phyllis, I think we're stranded." It was getting late and we were exhausted. "Phyllis, why don't we just get a hotel? This is Houston. We can get a hotel in town and figure this out in the morning when tire shops open back up."

She said, "No, let's keep trying. Let's go eat and figure this out." Now, that is a smart woman, because when you are feeling stranded, food always sounds good. We found the nearest Pappasito's, like any good Houstonian would do, and got an outside table. I was exhausted. At that point, I didn't even care about Galveston and the beach cabin. I was ready to just find a hotel and maybe go home the next day. I didn't know what to do.

Phyllis, however, wasn't ready to give up. She pulled out her phone and started making calls. We finally found an emergency roadside assistance company that had two brand new tires that fit our trailer. They could also come and install them. They were changing our tires before we finished eating. It was amazing. We ended up getting to the beach cabin late that night and woke up to enjoy the beach the next morning, just like we had originally intended.

We found out later that the original trailer tires were dry-rotted; they had been sitting stagnant for too long. When dry-rotted tires get hot or under too much pressure, they just explode. That's why it happened just a few miles away from our house.

But here's the part I don't want you to miss: *Those two blowouts almost caused us to settle in a place that we were supposed to pass through.*

I wonder if you've had some "blowouts" in your life that have caused you to settle in a place that you were supposed to just pass through. I wonder if certain situations in your life have been sitting stagnant or have dry-rotted, and now a little heat and pressure have caused something to blow in your marriage? I've heard people say, "Well, I'm having marriage problems because of Covid." No, Covid didn't cause their problems; it only magnified and exposed their problems.

When pressure exposes a problem, we need to take a step back and ask, "Why?" The pressure didn't create the problem; it exposed the problem, and now you've got a blowout. Maybe, like me, you feel stuck where you are. But you aren't stuck! This is what I know: God doesn't want you to settle in this place. He doesn't want you to settle where you are with a blowout. I'm here to encourage you like Phyllis encouraged me;

it's not time to settle! It's not time to stop. It's time to look for the open door God has prepared for you. I don't know about you, but I'm ready to pass through and not get stuck in a place that I was never intended to settle in.

Stuck in Pain

There's a story in Genesis 11 that I want to tell from a little different perspective than how others might tell it. It's the story where Abraham's father uproots his family to move from Ur of the Chaldees into the land of Canaan (Genesis 11:31-32). He takes his family—Abraham, Sarah, and Lot—and they head toward Canaan, but we are told that when they got to Haran, they settled there. Haran was a city between Canaan and Ur. They didn't pass through; they *settled*. What a powerful word. Then we are told that Terah lived two hundred and five years and died in Haran.

As I read the Bible, I try to put myself in the shoes of those I am reading about. Terah is no exception. We don't know why he settled in Haran because the Bible doesn't tell us. We simply know that he was moving his family to Canaan and settled in Haran.

Why did he do that? What would have caused him to settle and not move forward with his plan for his life? There are a lot of possible reasons, and we will never know for sure. However, I can think of two possibilities that might be the same reasons you or I would settle in our lives today. In Genesis 11:28, we see that Terah had a son named Haran who died before he left Ur. His son shared the same name of the city Terah was now in.

I think one reason Terah might have settled is that he got stuck in a place of pain. Josephus, the ancient historian, wrote, "Now Terah, hating Chaldea, on account of his mourning for Haran (his son), moved to Haran (the city)." We see that he was still mourning the loss of his son as he began his journey.

No parent should ever have to grieve the loss of a child. It doesn't matter how old the child is; the loss is devastating. As a pastor, I have had to officiate many funerals, and it's always tough to see people grieve the loss of a loved one, regardless of the circumstances. But the funerals that are the hardest for me personally are the ones when a parent must bury their child. It's devastating for all involved, especially the parents. Some parents never fully recover from this tragic loss, though thankfully for believers there is hope and comfort regardless of how painful the loss is—that one day we will all be reunited again in heaven for all of eternity with those we've lost.

Like Terah, one reason I see a lot of people settle is that they get stuck in a place of pain: the pain of loss, the pain of tragedy, the pain of disappointment, the pain of betrayal. The list could go on and on. It's easy to get stuck when you've experienced deep pain and trauma. The loss is real and it takes time to heal, recover, and move forward in life after something so traumatic. But too often, we allow smaller hurts and pains, things that shouldn't hold us up, to become blowouts that keep us on the side of the road of life.

One time I was wakeboarding on the lake at Camp Pine Cove with my family. Wakeboarding is not an easy sport, and we hadn't done it very much. That day, everyone in our group had taken a turn: my wife Phyllis, my sister-in-law Stephanie, my brother Steve, and then it was my turn.

Well, nobody else in our group had gotten up on their first try, but I was thinking "your boy" is going to be the first to do it. I was in the water, psyched up and ready to go. I was lying down, ready to pull myself up, and they were all laughing because I was practically drowning while trying to keep my foot in the holster and right-side up. I thought to myself, *I'm going to hold on to this rope if it's the last thing I do! If it kills me, I will not let go!* I was holding the handle as tight as I could as the boat took off. I was thinking, *Don't let go! Don't let go! Hold on!*

Well, I was holding on so hard and the pressure was so strong that suddenly the handle broke off and hit my hand! The force of the impact on my hand was so severe that the nail on my index finger immediately turned blue. I was in a lot of pain, yet my pride didn't allow me to tell everyone how badly I was hurt. The driver of the boat leaned over and yelled, "Let's go get another rope; you got this." They pulled me back into the boat and offered to get another rope so I could try again, but I declined. I came up with an excuse and recommended someone else try because our time on the water was limited. To this day, though, I have never tried to wakeboard again because of the pain of a random accident. The pain paralyzed me.

I wonder how often the same thing happens to us in life. Maybe you experienced traumatic pain as a child. Maybe you experienced abuse—verbal, physical, or even sexual. That pain and trauma of the past is real, and it can cause you to get stuck in some areas. Maybe you haven't moved past it, and it's affecting you today. Or more recently, maybe a spouse did something, your child said something, or the company you've been fiercely loyal to let you go—dropped you like a hot potato without even thinking twice. God forbid, but maybe the church is the source of your unresolved pain. Perhaps somebody didn't reach out to you or didn't acknowledge something you were going through. That new pain and rejection can trigger older, lingering pain, and it will rob God's best from your life. You have to allow God to help you! You have to say, "God, I've got some unresolved pain from my childhood [or from recent times], and I refuse to settle in a place I was called to pass through."

Stuck in Comfort

I think a second reason Terah might have settled is that he got stuck in a place of comfort. When you examine Terah and his family's path, they would have traveled six hundred miles to get to Haran. You can imagine he's exhausted. He's tired, and they have several hundred miles left to get to Canaan. Terah is an older man. This would have been a place of rest. He is no longer traveling over treacherous roads. He is safe and has found a new sense of security. Haran would have seemed familiar. The people there served the same moon god as the people in their former home of Ur. Terah, according to Jewish literature, was a craftsman who made idols. He may have found a blossoming trade in Haran. This seems to be upheld by scripture: "This is what the Lord, the God of Israel, says: 'Long ago your ancestors, including Terah the father of Abraham and Nahor, lived beyond the Euphrates River and worshiped other gods" (Joshua 24:2).[4] Even though Terah wasn't in Canaan, Haran may have been a whole lot better than the place he had left. It was comfortable. Even though it wasn't the place of promise God spoke to Abraham, Terah may have decided he could build a good life right where he was and settled in an area he intended to pass through.

I have found in my own life that it's hard to get motivated when I'm comfortable. As Christians, we must remember that heaven is our home. God comforts us here, but since we are citizens of heaven just passing through this existence on earth, God doesn't want us to get comfortable apart from Him. It's okay to have wealth, be blessed, and have nice things, but don't allow those earthly treasures to stop you from moving forward into God's purpose for your life. Don't allow the blessing to distract you and cause you to settle.

C.S. Lewis, the great scholar, said, "Prosperity knits a man to the world. He feels that he is 'finding his place in it' while really it is finding its place in him. His increasing reputation, his widening circle of acquaintances, his sense of importance, the growing pressure of absorbing and agreeable work, build up in him a sense of being really at home in earth."[5] I'm not speaking against prosperity and blessing. I believe God wants to bless us so that we can be a blessing to others. One of the ways God chooses to bless the world is by blessing His people. But what we must guard against is allowing wealth to make us complacent or comfortable and cause us to settle and not reach the place of promise in our lives.

Despite numerous obstacles of all types, the apostle Paul knew what it was like to keep moving forward. He considered all his previous earthly accolades as rubbish compared to knowing and pursuing Christ. He pressed on, forgetting what was behind him and reaching for what was ahead—the prize God had for him at the end of his journey (Philippians 3:12-14).

Paul is credited with writing thirteen or fourteen of the twenty-seven New Testament books. He had a lot to be proud of as a learned Jewish leader, and even more as a leader in the church. Yet despite his "bragging rights," never in his life did he say, "It's time to settle. I think I'll take it easy for a while."

No, he says, "I press on. I'm moving forward toward the goal to win the prize for which God has called me heavenward in Christ Jesus." And that should encourage us all: Don't let your life settle in a place you're supposed to pass through.[6]

Scan here to listen to my podcast episode, **"Don't Settle Where You Are,"** *as you continue your journey to being unstoppable.*

CHAPTER 4

A Life Without Regret

*Your best life is not an easy life,
but it's a significant life.*

Our life on this earth is short. But what we have to be cognizant of is the fact that we are all on a spiritual journey. It doesn't matter what you believe about religion or how spiritual you think you are or aren't. God created you. He hand-fashioned you. Ecclesiastes 3:11 says, "He has also set eternity in the human heart." Think about that for a minute. God actually deposited eternity into the heart of every person. That's why I can say with confidence that you are on a spiritual journey, with eternity in your heart.

Your life will never feel in sync or complete unless it's surrendered to God. That's why you can be rich, you can be successful, you can be intelligent, and you can reach all of your dreams, yet still feel empty inside. All of life's accomplishments are meaningless without God. It's tragic to see someone climb the ladder of success that the world said would make them happy, only to realize ... it didn't. Success didn't bring wholeness and happiness. They have a lot of "stuff," but the problem is that all of that "stuff" actually has them. They are stuck and bound to a system that will never satisfy. But all that can change in a minute. When God has us—our hearts, soul, mind, and emotions—that's when we can truly be happy.

I read a fascinating article about a lady named Bronnie Ware, an Australian nurse who spent several years taking care of patients during the last twelve weeks of their lives. She recorded their dying epiphanies in a book called *The Top Five Regrets of the Dying*. In the book, Ware writes of the phenomenal clarity of vision that people gain at the end of their lives and how we can learn from them. When questioned about any regrets they had or anything they would do differently, common themes surfaced again and again. Following are the top five regrets of the dying, as recorded by Ware.

When I read these top five regrets, I see the four foundational building blocks of life that if we address today, can make a difference over the span of our lifetime. We'll explore each of these in the coming chapters, but let's learn from those who have gone before us and turn things around now, so we won't have to die on a bed of regrets. Here are the top five regrets Ware discovered:

Regret #1:

"I wish I'd had the courage to live a life true to myself, not the life others expected me to live." Have you ever felt this way? Have you felt like you were spending your energy trying to be something you're not? When you learn to live according to your true identity, not according to others' expectations, you will overcome this regret.

Regret #2:

"I wish I hadn't worked so hard." Ware explains that all the men she took care of deeply regretted spending so much of their lives on the treadmill of a work existence. Why? There's nothing wrong with working hard. But when your time gets out of balance it's often because you don't truly understand your purpose. Your purpose is multidimensional—a concept we will explore later in this book. For now, just know that when you understand your purpose, you prioritize your time and efforts differently, so you don't end up with this regret.

Regret #3:

"I wish I'd had the courage to express my feelings."
Many people suppressed their feelings in order to keep peace with others and avoid confrontation. As a result, they settled for a mediocre existence and never became who they were truly capable of becoming. Sometimes our feelings get locked inside because of past pain and trauma. Maybe you tried to express yourself before, but it wasn't received. It's time to find healing and move past those stuck places and get a vision of what God has for your future. When you see who you are and understand that your expression adds value to the world around you, you will find the confidence to speak from your heart with no regrets!

Regret #4:

"I wish I had stayed in touch with my friends."
It can be easy to get so caught up in ourselves and our own existence that we let friendships slip by over the years. But when we really understand that our relationships are all that we have that last into eternity, we refocus on what is most important. I will address this in the last chapter of this book.

Regret #5:

"I wish I had let myself be happier." Many people did not realize until the end that happiness is a choice. They had stayed stuck in old patterns and habits. The so-called "comfort" of familiarity overflowed into their emotions as well as in their physical lives. This has everything to do with your internal paradigm—your internal programming and beliefs that either move you forward or keep you stuck in life.

God doesn't want us to carry the burden of regret. He wants us to live with understanding, purpose, and passion. Paul said it like this, "And let us run with endurance the race God has set before us. We do this by keeping our eyes on Jesus, the champion who initiates and perfects our faith" (Hebrews 12:1-2 NLT). It's God's desire that you not only start your race but finish it strong. He doesn't want you to lay your head to rest on a bed of regrets at the end of your life. He doesn't want you living on autopilot day in and day out, just going through the motions of life. He wants you to be fulfilled and satisfied, strong and spiritually unstoppable. When you are spiritually unstoppable, it means that nothing can or will stop you in your pursuit of Christ and fulfilling His purpose for your life, regardless of how difficult your circumstances become.

Four Foundational Building Blocks of Life

In life, we get stuck because we fail to discover, neglect, or lose sight of one or more of the four essential building blocks of life. Each of these building blocks is unique and requires time, energy, and focus:

1. **Identity:** who you are in Christ
2. **Purpose:** what you are supposed to be doing now
3. **Vision:** where you are going and/or a picture of the future
4. **Paradigm:** your conscious and subconscious pattern or habit of thought

Furthermore, God created each of us as a unique, multifaceted, complex reflection of himself (Genesis 1:27). Therefore, it's our responsibility to live up to the potential that God has placed inside of us. I want to help you do this by encouraging you to discover your identity, live with purpose, get a clear vision for where you're going, and cultivate a healthy, life-giving paradigm. It takes intentionality in all four of these areas to keep your life moving forward in the right direction, so we'll go into more detail about these building blocks in later chapters of this book.

Are you ready? Let's go on a journey to help you get unstuck and become unstoppable.

When God Came Looking for Me

"And what do you benefit if you gain the whole world but lose your own soul? Is anything worth more than your soul?" (Matthew 16:26 NLT).

There is a hunger deep inside each of us that longs to be satisfied. It's a void that many try to fill with all kinds of things that never satisfy: money, success, relationships, drugs, excessive alcohol, sexual promiscuity, entertainment, sports, etc. Some of these can seem harmless—and they are, in and of themselves. Problems arise, however, when you depend on them to satisfy the internal hunger that only God can satisfy. Apart from God, you will always feel like something is missing. You will feel incomplete and lacking. That's why it's only in a relationship with our Creator that we find true meaning and purpose for our lives.

In 2003, I found myself at the lowest point in my life. I was twenty-six years old, and Phyllis and I had been married for three years. We were a young, seemingly successful couple. My twin brother and I co-owned real estate properties in three local cities, and my wife and I owned and operated a restaurant that was gaining local fame. However, what people could not see is that in the midst of our success, our lives were falling apart. They were unraveling at the seams. After only three years, Phyllis and I were struggling to keep it all together, not only professionally but personally. Others saw us as the perfect couple. It wasn't uncommon for people to call us Ken and Barbie. We went to church regularly. We thought love and success and being good people were all that you needed to be happy and fulfilled in life. But we were both wrong. Internally, I was confused and frustrated and felt so lost.

The pressure of success and a dysfunctional marriage led us down a path of using drugs and alcohol to cope with our pain. I knew what we were doing was wrong, but instead of running to God, I ran away from Him. I felt like a fraud and a fake as I continued to project an image of success and happiness while I was dying on the inside. Our substance abuse started off innocently. We were at a friend's house one night, and he could tell I was stressed and frustrated, so he offered me some drugs to help me relax. He said that the drugs would help Phyllis and me reconnect, and he was right; they did. For a short while, all of the cares of life and struggles in our marriage faded away. However, when the drugs wore off, our problems were still there. Nothing had changed. Instead of dealing with our issues, we were simply masking our pain. At the time, I couldn't see it. I just wanted the pain to stop. We began partying occasionally. Then, every weekend. It wasn't long before we would go on five-day binges of drugs and alcohol—anything to numb this feeling of emptiness and hopelessness. Our lives were spiraling out of control.

It was February 7, 2003, the day I hit the lowest point in my life, that God came searching for me. Phyllis and I had been up for days partying, and at just past midnight I was in my bathroom getting ready to go out for the fifth night in a row, when all of a sudden God showed up.

I'll never forget how overwhelming His presence was. Even in my sin I felt his unconditional love. I began to have an open vision. I saw one road that split into two paths. One path led to heaven and the other path led to hell. Then, I heard the voice of God speak to me. He said, "This is your moment of decision." His voice wasn't audible, but it was so strong it felt audible. His words were piercing. I felt the weight of eternity. Heaven or hell. Which would I choose? In that moment, I was awakened to how lost I was in my soul, and I cried out to God. I came out of the bathroom, kicked everyone else out of our house, and Phyllis and I had a divine encounter with God that lasted for five hours. I have never been the same. Though I grew up in church and knew about God, I realized that I didn't know God. Though I had been raised in church, it didn't make me a Christian. I couldn't live off the faith of my family or my parents. That night I made the decision to follow Jesus for myself.

I believe someone is reading this book right now who is at that deciding point like I was. You may not be strung out on drugs or going out to party with friends, but you can relate to the overwhelming pressures of life. You can relate to making decisions that you are not proud of and realizing that you are not living the life that God created you to live. Maybe you feel lost and confused. Maybe you feel overwhelmed or are struggling with depression and anxiety. Maybe you're feeling the emptiness that comes from a life without God. It doesn't matter how successful you are or how much money you make or how many things you have; without God, it's all worthless. He is the only one who can give your life meaning and purpose. You can do what I did in that moment. I simply surrendered. For the next couple of hours, sitting in my bathroom, God spoke to me in a profound way. But it was the moment of surrender that changed my life. I chose to respond to His presence and power and surrender everything.

If that's you today, maybe you have been strung out on drugs, dependent on antidepressants, or drinking regularly just to cope with life. If you have found yourself in a hole like I was in, feeling lost or hopeless, or like your life is just a mess that you can't fix, why don't you surrender all to Him today? Please let me lead you in a prayer of surrender right now: Just say,

Lord, I bring You all of me, in exchange for all of You. I repent for sinning against You. Jesus, I believe You're the Son of God, that You died for my sins and on the third day You rose again. Today, and for the rest of my days, I commit to serving You, and to saying "yes" no matter what lies ahead. I confess that You are my God, my Savior, and my Lord. In Jesus' name, amen.

If you prayed that prayer, send me an email at mystory@jimnkyles.com

I want to hear what God has done in your life.

When You Define Him in Your Life as He Defines Himself, He Defines You

Jesus had twelve disciples that He mentored during His three years of ministry. During those years, He trained them and helped them uncover their identity, purpose, and vision for the future. He poured himself into their lives and helped them change their old way of thinking. He would often say things like, "You have heard it said, but I say..." He was challenging the norms of Jewish culture, religion, and thought of the day. He spoke life and truth into their hearts and led them on a journey to free them from their old way of thinking and living. They were not perfect, but overall, they kept growing day by day. In retrospect, we know that ultimately this ragtag group would change the world.

Other people who observed Jesus had a lot of different opinions about exactly who He was (Matthew 16:13-14). One day Jesus asked His disciples, "But who do you say I am?" Simon Peter responded: "You are the Messiah, the Son of the living God" (Matthew 16:15-16).

In response, Jesus replied, "You are blessed, Simon son of John, because my Father in heaven has revealed this to you. You did not learn this from any human being. Now I say to you that you are Peter (which means 'rock') and upon this rock I will build my church, and all the powers of hell will not conquer it" (Matthew 16:17-19 NLT).

I love Peter. Peter was a little rough around the edges, somewhat gritty and impulsive. Today, we might say he was kind of a thug. Peter gets a lot of flak, but he was the only disciple who stepped out of the boat to walk on water by faith when he saw Jesus. Out of passion to protect Jesus, he impulsively cut off the ear of one Jesus' opponents who had come to arrest Him in Gethsemane. (Jesus reattached the ear. He can heal the wounds that we cause others to experience due to our unbridled passion and ignorance.)

So here we see Peter again. He was the only one bold enough to reply to Jesus' question, "Who do you say that I am?" We know that later Peter denied Jesus, but after Pentecost he was also the one who stepped out of the upper room and preached the gospel boldly, and three thousand people experienced salvation in one day. We see Peter was all over the place, but in a moment that really counted, Peter affirmed, "You are the Messiah." This was a prophetic revelation that was a game changer because they all knew the Messiah was coming, but what they had only internalized was now publicly spoken. "You're the Messiah, Son of the living God," Peter replied. And then something unexpected happened. Jesus turned around and revealed who Peter was. Jesus said, "You are blessed, Simon son of John." Here Simon, son of John, would become Peter, the rock.

Jesus basically told him, "Now that you defined who I am, I'm going to define who you are: you are

Peter [a rock]." Jesus defined Peter, not by his past mistakes or present circumstances, but by his God-given identity. This was the real Peter, regardless of how he saw himself or how others tried to define him.

Understand that the revelation of who you are, your identity, is birthed out of your relationship with Jesus Christ. You are who He says you are—nothing more and nothing less.

The name Peter means "rock." Jesus was saying, "Peter, you're a rock." He was speaking about the rock of revelation that was inside him. The rock of revelation was twofold: number one, it was the revelation of who Jesus was, but number two, it was also the revelation of who Peter was and who he would become—his true identity. If you have an accurate revelation of who Jesus is and an accurate revelation of who you are, and those two working together, there's no devil in hell that can stop what God wants to do. Jesus adds that for the church He would be building upon that rock of revelation, the gates of hell would not prevail against it.

So now we know that even when Peter made a mistake, he went back to the revelation of his identity spoken over him by Jesus. He remembered, "But I'm a rock." Yes, after denying Christ, he had a momentary lapse of who he was and returned to his old life of fishing, but he didn't stay there for long. Jesus showed up on the shore, reminded him of who he was, and Peter reengaged in the mission.

Even though he got stuck and went back to his old life, he didn't stay there because his identity pulled him into the upper room, pulled him into the presence of God, and pulled him to the place where he needed to be. On Pentecost, he was filled with power from the Holy Spirit and came out and preached the gospel fearlessly.

Your Best Life Is Not an Easy Life, It's a Significant Life

Like Peter, we each have to decide: Will I live for myself and face one or more of those five significant regrets toward the end of life? Or will I live my life, my best life, for the one I have confessed as my Savior?

Your best life, living for your Savior, will not be without opposition. You will face challenges and must stand against the devil, but the reality is by doing so you're also going to impact heaven. That's what your best life is all about: a significant life. Don't look for the easy life; look for the significant life. Have the attitude that says, "God, I'll fight any battle You want me to fight. God, I'll go anywhere You want me to go and do anything You want me to do because I know that what's inside of me, You placed inside of me, because the world needs it."

When the world sees us living the victorious life that God created us to live, that's when they will say, "God, I want to be like them. How did you do that? How did you get through that?" And then we become salt and light to the world around us. We need to walk around in victory, letting the world see that God is real.

Scan here for your free assessment to help you overcome your regrets.

CHAPTER 5

Are You Held Captive?

God created you with a great purpose and destiny,
and He hardwired you to be free.

I read an article once about elephants living in captivity and how their trainers "domesticated" or trained them. I was fascinated by the article because an elephant can easily crush a human. An elephant is so strong that it can uproot an entire tree. It can knock down buildings and homes and even flip a car with ease. They are big and powerful, and they also love to roam free. Elephants are meant to be anything but held captive!

How do the trainers domesticate an animal so big and powerful? The process is simple but effective. When the elephant is still a baby, they tie a chain or a thick rope to its ankle and then tie the other end of that rope to a tree. The baby elephant's natural inclination is to be free. But now it's got this rope around its ankle, tied to this tree. When it tries to walk around—to do what it was created to do—it cannot go anywhere. Because the elephant is small, it can't break the rope, no matter how hard it tries. Eventually, one day the elephant makes up its mind that breaking free is impossible. An internal shift takes place. That little elephant gives up on fulfilling its own natural desire to roam and be free. Its will is broken. The elephant is forever changed from the inside out. And for the rest of the elephant's life, it will never try to break free again, no matter how big or how old it gets. That's why you can go to the circus and see this massive elephant held by a small rope tied to a little stake in the ground, and that elephant doesn't even try to break free. This massive, majestic, strong animal doesn't even know what it's capable of because it is held back by the chains of past trauma.

I wonder if that's not a picture of what happens to those of us who follow Jesus. As a believer you are spiritually powerful; you are mighty and strong in Christ. God created you with a great purpose and destiny, and He hardwired you to be free. Yet because of the chains of the past and adverse childhood experiences, you've become captive. That trauma prevents you from living life the way God intended for you to live. Gradually, you've given up hope of breaking free of the chains that have you bound because you don't even know it's possible. I want you to know that regardless of your past and the chains that have held you captive, you're not the same person you were when that happened. You're older, more mature, stronger, wiser, more capable; you're growing. You are more powerful than you think and you have full access to what you need to experience the freedom of God in every area of your life.

Possibility Beyond the Pain

If there were awards for people who experienced the most pain and trauma in life, the apostle Paul would certainly be a winner. Of course, it's not a competition, but when we look at what others have been through, his suffering helps us get a new perspective. It helps us see the possibility again. Here's a snapshot of just a few things Paul experienced after his conversion:

I have worked much harder, been in prison more frequently, been flogged more severely, and been exposed to death again and again. Five times I received from the Jews the forty lashes minus one. Three times I was beaten with rods, once I was pelted with stones, three times I was shipwrecked, I spent a night and a day in the open sea, I have been constantly on the move. I have been in danger from rivers, in danger from bandits, in danger from my fellow Jews, in danger from Gentiles; in danger in

*the city, in danger in the country, in danger at sea;
and in danger from false believers. I have labored
and toiled and have often gone without sleep; I
have known hunger and thirst and have often
gone without food; I have been cold and naked.*
—2 Corinthians 11:23–27

When I read this list, I know I have nothing to
complain about. But the most amazing thing is that
in the midst of all of his trials and struggles, the
apostle Paul knew how to move his life forward.
Over and over again we see Paul's uncanny ability to
handle adversity in the right way. Paul didn't become
bitter. He wasn't angry; he didn't get offended; he
wasn't resentful. Paul didn't just endure the pain
and suffering and do what was right because he had
to. He embraced the struggle as he overcame the
challenges in his life, realizing that each challenge
he faced was an opportunity to bring God glory. Even
when his suffering didn't make sense, he responded
with strength and grace.

God is not simply looking for compliance from
us. He's looking for willing obedience, and there is a
difference. We've all heard the story about the student
who wouldn't sit down. The teacher asked again and
again, "Please sit down," but the student repeatedly

refused. Only after the teacher threatened to call the student's parents did the student finally comply: "All right, I'll sit down, but I'm standing up on the inside." Spiritually, that's what compliance looks like for many people. That's our response to the challenges of our life. "Okay, God, I'll do what You say if You're going to make me." Or we barter with God: "God, if you'll do this, I'll do that." But God doesn't want you to obey because you have to—like you don't have any other options. God wants your heart to be surrendered to Him because you know that He is good. The heart of surrender says, "I am going to do what You asked because I love you, not because I have to."

God wants us to embrace His will for our lives, whether we like it or not, whether we understand it or not, whether it's easy or not. He wants us to trust Him and to trust that He has our life in His hands. And here's what I know: Whatever happens, no matter how tough or how bad, if you have the right attitude, the right heart, the right mindset, God can turn your situation around. He can use what the enemy meant to destroy you as a divine setup for you to fulfill your purpose (Romans 8:28).

No More Excuses

People look at the heroes of the faith—the men and women of the Bible—and think they are superhuman. I have often thought as much. There is no way they could experience such extreme circumstances and still remain so strong and resilient. However, verses like James 5:17 tell us that our heroes of the faith were just normal everyday people like you and me. If that's the case, then what did they know that I don't? If they were just like you and me, how could they live life and keep everything moving forward? What was different? What secret did they know?

They learned the secret of living, which Paul hints at in Philippians 4:12 (NLT): "I know how to live on almost nothing or with everything. I have learned the secret of living in every situation, whether it is with a full stomach or empty, with plenty or little." I love how Paul gives us the opposite extremes in these examples. He wants us to know that he can relate to us whether we are rich or poor, whether our bellies are full or empty, whether we have a lot or a little. He's leading up to a secret he wants to share with all of us—one that works in every situation. Here's his secret: "I can do everything through Christ, who gives me strength" (Philippians 4:13 NLT).

Please get this: the context of this great truth is that whether we have a little or a lot, we can move forward because it is Christ who strengthens us, not our circumstances. These ten words unlock the mystery that many spend their lives hoping to discover. It's here that we see Paul is able to overcome the challenges of life because of the strength that comes from a relationship with Jesus Christ. After my salvation experience, I, too, would come to learn the power of Christ's sustaining strength in me regardless of my circumstances.

At first, life was great. Phyllis and I went back to church and our relationship began to experience healing and restoration. Our real estate was doing well and our restaurant business was booming. We were even expanding operations at the restaurant because of the growth and increase. Life was good. That's why what happened next was so unexpected. Six months later, the restaurant would be unjustly shut down by the landlord. He made a false accusation of nonpayment of rent; however, by the time we were able to go to court to regain entry to the property, we had lost our inventory, our employees, and our reputation. But it didn't stop there. Multiple tenants from our rental properties moved out for different reasons. Now, with no other income, we were in trouble. Several of our houses were headed into foreclosure. We were behind with the payments on our car, and it was about to be repossessed.

I was frustrated and mad at God. How could this be happening to us? It was then that I read Philippians 4:13 and realized that regardless of what I was walking through, my strength comes from my relationship with Christ. The fact that Paul's revelation applied to my life didn't make the difficulty of my situation go away. However, it did give me the strength to do what Paul did, to overcome the challenges. Ultimately, it was a hard season where we witnessed God's miraculous provision for us day by day. Supernaturally, we never lost a house or a car. We never went without food or the basic necessities of life. It was then that I learned how to lean on His strength through relationship with Him.

Second, as mentioned, it was Paul's faithful mindset that helped propel him forward. It was his firm belief that when things got hard, he could get through the tough times based on Christ's strength. When he was shipwrecked, he said, "I can ... through Christ." When he was beaten, he said, "I can ... through Christ." When things were going good, he said, "I can

… through Christ." His mentality was based on his faith in Christ's power in all situations.

It's time to stop making excuses. I have learned that excuses only validate your reality. Excuses are what we use when we want to justify our point of view about why something can't be done. Yes, it's true that your perspective matters, but just remember that your perspective is only one of many points of view. God has a point of view for your circumstances as well.

If you are not careful, your excuses will keep you chained to the pain of the past, oblivious even to the power of Christ in you. Remember the elephants. Your excuses keep you from moving past fear. God is trying to help you break free from the chains of the past that have limited your life. He is trying to break the mentality from the enemy that says, "You can't … because." God says, "You can!"

Having an "I can through Christ" mentality is something that I have worked hard to develop in my own life and instill into my family. We have a rule at our house that the Kyles family is not allowed to say the two words, "I can't." Those words are simply unacceptable in our house. If anyone happens to say it, the immediate response is, "We don't say 'I can't.' Kyles can." Even on occasions when I have found myself saying, "I can't," my kids will correct me and say, "No, Dad, Kyles can."

> Excuses only validate
> your reality.

This simple shift in mentality has radically changed my life and our family. It opens up a world of possibilities because if you think you can, then you will. Whatever you are trying to do, you eventually will do it because you believe you can. The moment you say, "I can't," you shut yourself off from all possibility of doing whatever it is you were trying to do. But when you think, "I can," now it becomes possible. Even if what you are trying to do seems impossible, instead of saying, "I can't," turn to God and say, "God, with You, I can do all things. What do You need me to do? How is this going to happen?" Make a quality decision to believe God's Word over your own opinion, and say "I can" with the strength that comes from Jesus Christ.

*Scan here to download your assessment to determine
if you are being held captive.*

CHAPTER 6

Life's Battlefield

We don't get stuck in life because of what happens to us, but because of what happens in us.

Not long ago, I was heading to the church office on my way from a doctor's appointment in Sugar Land, about twenty-five minutes away. I was excited about my afternoon and thinking about some things I wanted to get done. It had been a great day, but all that changed in a matter of moments.

I was in my truck, which is no ordinary truck. It's a Ford F-150 that has a six-inch rough country lift, twenty-inch rims and thirty-five-inch mud tires. I love my truck and I enjoy driving it. That day I was approaching a red light and slowed down like I normally do, by pushing on the brakes. As I came to a stop, my front wheels suddenly froze up. Thankfully, I wasn't driving fast, so the truck stopped right at the white line before the light. But something wasn't right. How could this be? I'd recently bought the truck and had only had it for two months. When I pushed the gas pedal, nothing happened. All kinds of questions were going through my mind. *What in the world has just happened to my truck? What do I do? Did the transmission just go out? Are the tires so big that the transmission dropped?* I was freaking out because the light was about to change at any moment and I wasn't sure I could move. I'd be that guy that everybody starts honking at, stopped at the green light with cars piling up behind me! I didn't deserve to be honked at like that. It's not like I was distracted or looking at my phone. I was sitting there legitimately having a technical problem with my new truck.

I continued sitting there pushing the gas pedal, and the car wouldn't go anywhere, so I pushed harder. *Come on! I'm not getting stuck!* I thought. *Jesus, help me!* Then I thought, *Okay, I have two options. I can sit here and look stupid, or I can just slam on the gas and go for it.* I gunned it, there was a loud pop, and the truck started moving forward. I was thinking, *Oh, praise God! Now my truck is going, but it's still acting funny.* I kept trying to figure out what was going on. I thought it might be an issue with the brakes, so I pulled into the next parking lot, pushed the brakes, and it did the exact same thing. The front wheels locked up.

I had no idea what to do at this point, so I talked to God, who I'm certain is just as concerned about my reputation as I am. I told Him, "I'm too old to be stranded or stuck! I mean, I'm not that old, but I'm just not going out like *that!*" I kept talking it through with myself and with God. *Okay, what if I put it in reverse? If it reverses, can it be the transmission? It's got to be the transmission. Come on, try it again, Jimbo. Come on, Jimbo! Come on, Jimbo. You can do it!* Again, I tried hitting the gas hard, and I heard another loud pop; however, the truck moved forward.

This time I was not stopping until I got to my destination, the church office, driving five to ten miles per hour with my hazard lights on all the way. I was going painfully slow. Cars were lining up behind me. I could only imagine what those drivers were thinking. "What's wrong with this guy? He's got this beautiful, nice, big new truck." I was concerned that something could fall apart at any moment. Finally, I pulled into the parking lot of our office. My assistant called a tow service to come and haul my truck to a repair shop.

About an hour or so later, the tow truck arrived and the driver asked me, "What's wrong?" I told him the story and he told me, "Get in the truck, turn the wheel, and let me get under there to take a look."

As soon as he got under my truck and started looking around, I heard him say, "Oh, I got it!"

I said, "Wow, really?" He said, "Yeah. Look, it's simple. The bolt that holds the brake pad to the rim of your truck fell out of place. It appears that when they put the new rims on, they didn't tighten the bolt and lock it into place, so the vibration of driving caused it to fall out."

The good news was, it was a simple fix. The bad news was that I was stuck and had to replace the rim due to the damage caused by the brake pad. Something as little as a loose screw kept my new truck from moving forward. Isn't it amazing how something so little can cause something so big to get stuck?

The Song of Solomon tells us that the small foxes are what spoil the vines (2:15). Little things can take us off course in big ways. This is especially true when it comes to our thoughts. The Bible says that our minds are a battlefield (2 Corinthians 10:3-5). We need to take very seriously the thoughts we allow to roll around in our minds. The wrong thoughts can lodge in our minds and cause us to get stuck in life. We often look for something major to blame for being the culprit of all our problems when it's the little things that can plague us the most. Our thoughts become the foundation for our beliefs, which produce our actions.

Your Thoughts Determine Your Future

In 2005, the National Science Foundation published an article summarizing research on human thought. It was found that the average person has about 12,000 to 60,000 thoughts per day. Of those thousands of thoughts, eighty percent were negative, and ninety-five percent were exactly the same repetitive thoughts as the day before.[7]

We can see that one of the strongest tendencies of our mind is to focus on the negative. It's no wonder people often feel stuck. Whatever you allow to fill your mind, whether positive or negative, will eventually show up in your life. That's why it's so important to meditate on the Word of God and His power as well as to think about what His purpose and plan are for your life.

Your thoughts compound day after day, month after month, year after year. Here's the good news: if you don't like what's happening in an area of your life, you can change it by changing your thoughts in that area. This is one of the most profound truths we can learn in life. It allows us to regain control of our lives. I don't have to be a victim of my circumstances or the environment around me. It doesn't matter what happens to me; I get to choose the course of my life by choosing my thoughts. This is why the Bible tells us to renew our minds according to the Word of God (Romans 12:2).

You and I are the builders of our own lives. Some might argue, "No, God's the Master Builder, right?" Yes, that's true in a spiritual sense because He gives us His blueprint for life through the Bible. Though God is great and powerful, He will not build your life for you. No, you are the one who builds your life by choosing what you think and do. God is a partner who gives us the master plan and fills us with His grace, which is His power and desire to do His will; however, you are the one who gets to do the work. The Bible says we work out our own salvation (Philippians 2:12). We work out what He works in. We build our own lives, and it starts with the thoughts we think.

We Don't Get Stuck in Life Because of What Happens to Us, but Because of What Happens in Us

Your thoughts determine your actions, and each action you take builds the foundation for your future. We saw that in the previous chapter when we looked at Paul's shipwreck. He didn't choose to focus on his circumstances. He chose to focus on God. We saw his perspective summed up: "I can do all things through Christ who strengthens me" (Philippians 4:13). No matter what challenge Paul faced, he knew he could face anything and do everything through the strength of Christ. His focus was on God and what He could do, and not on himself and what he couldn't do.

The direction of your focus, whether on self or on God, determines the direction of your life. We can either focus on what's going wrong in life or on what God can do in the midst of our circumstances. But it's very important where we choose to set our focus and which thoughts we allow ourselves to meditate on. That's why 2 Corinthians 10:5 tells us to "take captive every thought to make it obedient to Christ."

Think about what Paul is telling us. He is saying that it's important not to let even one inappropriate thought just flippantly hang out in your mind. Wow, that's a powerful truth and it takes a lot of work. Many people struggle because they lack the discipline to live the life God has called us to. If everyone could do it, if it were easy, then everybody would do it. The Bible doesn't promote doing things that are easy. It challenges us to do things that will have an eternal impact on our lives and the lives of the people around us. God wants our lives to be lived in such a way that heaven is brought to earth, so the world can see and know that He is real. He wants us to populate heaven and thereby reduce the future population of hell, and let me tell you, that's not an easy thing. Why? Because the devil is constantly planting seeds of doubt and unbelief in our hearts through unbiblical, often negative thoughts in our minds. He wants you to get stuck and wants to keep you stuck, but when you are diligent and stand on guard against him, you will win every time.

One of the most vulnerable times is when you are left alone with your unfiltered and unguarded thoughts. It happens to all of us, right? For me, that's when I'm driving. One time I was driving down Benton Road at a railroad crossing, about to pass through the light. I wasn't intentionally thinking about anything. (My wife tells me she doesn't understand how that's possible.) But then something started meddling in my mind. I was frustrated at a personal conflict earlier that day and, lo and behold, the enemy started dropping negative thoughts in my head about the other person. Those thoughts became so strong that I started having an argument with that person in my head! I was literally saying in my mind, "No, you don't know what you're talking about!" Then I mentally started telling the person off. My imagined argument was so real I could feel my blood pressure rising and I started to get angry. My driving became a little more aggressive than before. I was frustrated. Here I was, sitting in my car alone, but I thought I knew how this other person was going to respond. Then I decided how I was going to respond in return.

I had imagined a whole conversation in my head by the time I finally arrived at my destination. Then, as I arrived, I saw this person. Before thinking, I spoke to him in frustration—before he even said or did anything to me! I was all worked up because of my mental conversation before I arrived. I had to remind myself that the conversation I had in my head wasn't real, and then ask for forgiveness. My frustration was unfounded and unwarranted.

The challenge and the tragedy of that moment is that God surely brought that person to my mind to create an opportunity for healing in our relationship. God probably wanted me to pray for the person, and to have a forgiving heart. Maybe He was even going to vindicate me by having that person apologize. God's priority is healing and restoration, but I allowed ungodly thoughts to fester in my mind without casting them down. I didn't refute the lies in that moment. I gave place to the enemy by dwelling on them and then opening my mouth in frustration, all because my thoughts were unguarded and unfiltered. That's why you have to catch yourself and be aware of what you are thinking about. You have to develop a disciplined thought life—day in and day out, night in and night out—to really live the life God purposes for you and find the freedom He intends. This is what Scripture means when it says, "Take captive every thought."

Thoughts Can Be Barriers or Building Blocks

Our thoughts are the building blocks of our lives. Our thoughts govern our actions. What we think can become a self-fulfilling prophecy. If you think and believe your marriage will never get better, what happens? You often don't bother putting in the work to get the result you really want: a healthy marriage. Because of your ungodly thoughts, you don't put intention or action in that direction. You don't put your faith in God for that healing. You close off the door to that potential.

However, when you pray and believe it will get better, you open the door to what God can do. Your faith is set on God and following His direction. You still have to put the work in to see the potential realized, but you are willing to do it because you know that with God, all things are possible (Matthew 19:26).

Your thoughts are the starting point to get you going in the right direction. You can apply this concept to every area of your life: work, finances, family, health, spiritual life, etc. Your thoughts either propel you forward into the eternal paradigm or hold you back in the temporal paradigm.

Roger Bannister was the first man to run a mile in under four minutes. Before 1954, it was believed that it was impossible for any runner to run a mile in less than four minutes. The prevailing mindset was that this was physically impossible and, if achieved, would lead to the death of the runner. It was thought that a human being simply couldn't run that fast. "Experts" conducted all sorts of profound studies to show it was absolutely impossible to beat the four-minute barrier. And for centuries, they were right. Nobody ever ran a mile in less than four minutes.

However, Roger Bannister believed he could break that barrier. He didn't dwell on the impossibilities. He refused to let all those negative words form a barrier or stronghold in his mind. He simply began to train, believing he was going to break that record, and sure enough, he went out one day and broke the four-minute-mile barrier. He did what the experts said couldn't be done. He made history. We know now that it wasn't a physical barrier, but a mental barrier.

Now, here is what is so interesting about the Roger Bannister story: Within ten years after Roger Bannister broke that record in 1954, 336 other runners had broken the four-minute-mile record as well! For three thousand years, as far back as statisticians kept track-and-field records, nobody ran a mile in less than four minutes. Then, within a decade, more than three hundred people from various geographical locations were able to do it. What happened? Simple. The barrier was in the athlete's mind all along. For all those years, runners believed what the experts were telling them. They were convinced that it was impossible to run a mile in less than four minutes. Roger Bannister had the right mentality. He refused to believe that it was impossible.

Now, think about your own life for a minute. What limits have you imposed on yourself because you believed what other people have said? Where have you allowed the limitations of others' experiences to become your own? If you are not careful, you can become trapped by your thinking and develop what is called a mental stronghold. This is a mindset that becomes impregnated with hopelessness and causes a believer to accept something as unchangeable, even though he or she knows it is contrary to the will of God.

Satan wants to trick you into believing that your situation is unchangeable or hopeless even though God's word says the opposite. Refuse to believe his lies and choose to trust that "Everything is possible for one who believes" (Mark 9:23). The choice to either believe the devil's lies or God's promises is your choice to make.

If You Want to Change Your Life, Change Your Thoughts

"Guard your heart above all else, for it determines the course of your life" (Proverbs 4:23 NLT).

Your heart is the core of who you are, which is determined by your thoughts. If you want to change your life, begin by changing your thoughts. Think about it. Two different people can go through a devastating, horrible tragedy. It derails one person for the rest of his life. He becomes a drug addict, goes to jail, becomes unproductive, alone, and isolated. Another person goes through something similarly devastating, but pulls through. Sure, it's difficult, but she grows through it.

She becomes better, not bitter. Maybe there's even a moment where God plants the seed of a dream of how she can make a difference in the lives of others. That tragedy becomes a turnaround moment—one that began with a different perspective and the direction of thoughts.

This is what happened to Hal Donaldson. He and his siblings were inspired to create a nonprofit organization when he was just twelve years old. One tragic night, a drunk driver crashed into his parents' vehicle. His father died in the crash, and his mother was disabled for a period of time. Their family didn't have food, clothes, or basic necessities. However, family and friends responded with love and assistance by providing clothing, food, and all the supplies the family needed.

As they got back on their feet, Hal and his siblings reflected on the impact others had made on their lives, and they wondered if they could do the same for other people. They saw others going through stressful, challenging tragedies and asked, "Can we feed them? Can we clothe them? Can we bring them disaster relief?" They got together and decided, "I think we can do it." Their plan eventually became Convoy of Hope. Today, Convoy of Hope has helped over 115 million people in more than fourteen different countries by providing food, water, and emergency supplies.

One person's pain leads to destructive behavior; another person's pain leads to a life of purpose. It largely hinges on their thoughts, which then direct the course of their life. You have no control over what happens *to* you, but you do get to choose what happens *in* you. It's so important to guard your thoughts. You must choose the direction of your thoughts with intentionality. You can't live your life on autopilot.

A recent study commissioned by Marks & Spencer determined that ninety-six percent of the three thousand people surveyed were living life on autopilot.[8] Ninety-six percent are going through the motions of life, day in and day out. There is an epidemic of non-engagement in our culture today. People have become comfortable going through life without much conscious thought, completely unaware of how they have relinquished their lives to the automatic programming of subconscious temporal thought. Most people go from one situation to another, rarely taking control of life and blind to eternal realities. They bounce around from one situation to the next, becoming victims of whatever circumstances impact them. This is living life on autopilot, with no intentionality, no goals, no drive. It's like a self-driving car that one might see driving around town. A person may be sitting in the driver's seat, but only to go along with the program, passively observing the world going by. Someone is there, but merely as a disengaged passenger.

> You have no control over
> what happens *to* you,
> but you do get to choose
> what happens *in* you.

Maybe as you read this, you recognize this is how you've been living. Although you are sitting in the driver's seat, you have relinquished control. You are no longer engaged in the process, but are simply along for the ride. Have you become nothing more than a spectator in your own life? If that's you, it's time to take back control and reengage. Together, let's go on a journey to discover truth about yourself and ultimately achieve freedom.

Scan here to watch my message, **"Life's Battlefield."**

CHAPTER 7

Discovering Your Identity

People define you by how they meet you, but God defines you by how He made you.

We hear a lot about identity theft these days. The idea that someone who is not you can pretend to be you is alarming. But even more alarming is you walking around not living as the real you because you don't know who you are.

To understand identity better, we must first realize there are two types of identity: self-identity and group or cultural identity. In this chapter I am going to focus on self-identity, which we will simply call identity. Your identity is more than just your name or what you do. According to *Psychology Today*, your identity encompasses the memories, experiences, relationships, and values that create your sense of self.[9]

As a Christian, your identity is more than this. It's not just who you are at your natural core but who you are in Christ Jesus (Ephesians 2:10). If we never realize that truth, then our journey to discover our identity will be flawed from the start. If you don't acknowledge who you are according to God's Word, you will allow what you do and the people around you to define you. Your self-assessed value and worth will be determined by external factors like your job title, financial status, friends, etc. Your self-worth and value will be in a constant state of flux based on your current condition and situation in life. People define you by how they meet you, but God defines you by how He made you.

Early in life, I received validation from the success of my businesses. If my businesses were doing well, I felt good. My value and self-worth were wrapped up in my success, and so was my self-esteem. Even today as a pastor, if I am not careful, I can find my value and worth wrapped up in how well our church is doing: how many new visitors we have, the number of small groups launched, the number of people assimilated into our discipleship program and serve teams, and so forth. It's easy to define yourself by external factors. Men tend to define themselves by the success of their accomplishments and status, whereas women tend to define themselves by the success of their relationships. This isn't an absolute, of course, but it's a general tendency.

It was shortly after I surrendered my life to Jesus Christ in 2003 that I hit the lowest point of my life. Not only had I lost my business, but also my marriage was falling apart. As I described briefly in Chapter Five, we were financially broke and about to lose everything we had worked so hard for. Four of our rental properties were headed into foreclosure. Our tenants in those properties all moved out at the same time. Our cars were just weeks away from being repossessed, even though I was working three jobs to try to make ends meet.

Have you ever heard the saying, "When it rains it pours"? Well, it was pouring, and I felt like I was drowning. Even though I was born again and God had radically changed me, my life was tough. I was doing everything I knew to do to keep us from losing everything and filing bankruptcy. I was frustrated and angry. I felt like I had done everything right. How could this happen to me? Hopelessness and depression began to set in. I couldn't see any way out of the darkness and started sinking deep into isolation. It was like a fog began to consume my life, and I couldn't see through it. I felt lost, afraid, and abandoned by God.

It was during this time that my mom asked my twin brother and me to attend a life-enrichment program.

It was a weekend encounter designed to help people experience inner healing. She had connected with the organization years earlier and volunteered as a facilitator for the program. At first, I declined, but after her persistent nudging, I thought, *What do I have to lose? I'm miserable anyway.* So my brother, Steve, and I decided to go. I didn't know what to expect, and frankly, I mostly just wanted to get my mom off my back. The first night, I was disappointed in my decision to attend. However, on the second day, something happened that would set the course of my life. I had no idea I was in the middle of a divine setup.

It was a Saturday, mid-morning, and we were told that we were going on a treasure hunt. We were to break away from the group and go somewhere by ourselves. A facilitator would then pass out a sheet of paper with a question that we were to answer. I thought, *No big deal. I can answer this question quickly and turn it back in so that I can take a break.* However, when I received the piece of paper and began to read the question, I felt paralyzed. I'd never had someone ask me this question before. And though it was a simple question, there was nothing simple about the answer. The question on the paper simply read, "Who am I?" I thought, *Who am I? That's so stupid. I know who I am.*

Most of the time when someone asks "Who are you?" they are asking about your name or what you do. But this time, the question went deeper. This question was not asking me about my external identification or occupation; this was an internal question focused on the core of who I was.

"Who are you?" I stared at the question with frustration. *What in the world does this mean?*

I flagged down one of the facilitators and said, "I don't understand the question." She simply asked me the question back. I repeated myself: "I don't understand what you are asking me." She asked it again. I shot back in frustration, "I am an entrepreneur and I'm a business owner."

"No. That's not who you are; that's what you do. *Who are you?*"

I pondered her question in frustration. I tried to dig deep and get honest with myself, and these words shot out of my mouth: "I'm a failure. I'm lost. I'm hopeless!"

"No. That's not who you are; that's how you *feel in your current condition*. Who are you, apart from what you do and how you feel? Think about it."

I had never thought about this question before. *Who are you, Jimn?* Honestly, I didn't know who I was. My identity had been so wrapped up in what I did that I couldn't answer the question. I sat there for what seemed like hours, pondering and trying to dig deep, but I continued to come up empty. Then I flagged down the facilitator again and said, "I am stuck. I don't know how to answer this question." With compassion and gentleness, she said, "Think about who created you. Why don't you pray and ask God to help you see who you are. God wants to reveal this to you, and He will if you'll ask Him to. Then after praying, just write down everything that comes to your mind. Write unfiltered and see what comes out."

I did just what she said. I prayed a simple prayer that forever set the course of my life. It went something like this, "God, please help me discover who I am. I feel lost and hopeless and confused, and I need you. *Please* help me see what You see so that I can become who You want me to be."

Shortly after that prayer, I began to write down what came to my mind, unfiltered. Words flowed onto the page, one sentence after another, and when there was nothing left to write, I dropped my pen. It was a surreal moment of clarity for me. I was excited, yet nervous. It was like discovering a hidden treasure buried in a field. I knew this was special, but I didn't know how special. I began rereading the sentences

I'd written down. *Wow! Is this really me? Have I just discovered who I am?* I read and then reread, again and again. Tears filled my eyes. It was so clear and yet so hidden. How could I have lived my whole life and never discovered this until now? It took this concentrated time away to focus on myself and begin to see myself the way God sees me.

I read it yet again, but this time thoughts of doubt rushed into my mind. All the failures and defeats from my past flooded my mind. *This is not who I am; there is no way. I am a failure. I am unqualified. I am undisciplined, and for sure, I am not a leader. I don't even have anything to lead anymore.*

It was in this moment of doubt and unbelief that I felt God speak to my heart: *This is you, Jimn. I made you and I fashioned you and formed you in your mother's womb. You can't run from who you are* (Psalm 139:13-14). Tears filled my eyes as God's words pierced my heart. It was the first time in my life I knew the real me. I discovered my identity didn't come from my position or title in life. It didn't come from my socioeconomic status or circle of friends, nor was it determined by my family. Instead, God was defining me and my value.

Then the facilitator asked everyone in our group, one by one, to stand up and share their identity statement. Each participant stepped up and began to share a statement of who they were. It was amazing to watch their faces light up as each person shared from their heart. There was a genuine discovery that had taken place. No one was trying to impress anyone; they each had a new understanding of their real, authentic identity. I knew my turn was coming up next. My hands began to sweat. My legs were shaky. I could feel my body tensing up. I was about to have to share something raw and vulnerable—something I had just discovered about myself minutes ago. Part of me was excited, yet I was so anxious and nervous. How would they respond? Would they validate my discovery, or would they just laugh and judge me or call me crazy? I had a choice to make. Would I boldly declare who I was, or shrink back and allow fear to cripple me and squelch the truth inside me?

It was finally my turn. The facilitator asked, "Jimn, would you please share with us your identity statement?" My brother also encouraged me, "Come on Jimn, you've got this." He knows me better than anyone, and he could tell I was nervous. I mustered up the courage to begin to declare my newly discovered identity statement from deep within me: "I am a general ..." I paused and hesitated. My courage quickly turned to fear as I felt all eyes peering in my direction. Even in my hesitation and insecurity, my brother Steve continued to cheer me on, "Come on Jimn; you've got this. You've got this. Come on, tell them who you are." I continued, "I am a general ..." When I finished sharing in the safety and privacy of that small-group setting, a huge weight lifted off me and I felt free. I felt full. I felt alive. I felt like my authentic self. I was forever changed.

I can't really put into words what happened that day. The only thing I know is that apart from my salvation moment, understanding my true identity was the most impactful moment of my life. I felt the smile of God as He filled my heart and mind with clarity. There was a new hope that filled my heart in a way that I can't explain. The darkness of my current circumstances began to fade away as I realized that what I was going through didn't affect who I was. My identity doesn't change; it's grounded in God and not in my circumstances. He is the one who created me. And since He is the one who made me, He was the only one who can define me. Therefore, my value is in Him and not in what I do. I had felt there was something great inside me my whole life, but no matter what I did, I could never seem to tap into it. But now, for the first time, a strength and grounding came from within that no one or nothing could ever take away.

Yes, later there would be seasons in my life in which I would have to remind myself of who I was daily, but ultimately my identity became my anchor, regardless of the challenges I was facing. Finally, I had what I needed to hold steady in the middle of life's storms.

I didn't realize the impact of that moment and how it would come to shape my life until many years later. But after the event, I would read my identity statement daily. I hung it on my mirror and framed it in my office. I would find myself saying it repeatedly, reaffirming who I was. At first, I felt like a fraud, or like I was reading someone else's identity—someone I admired and looked up to—yet how could that be? My life was anything but admirable. I had just lost my business and my marriage was still struggling. (Salvation doesn't instantly fix this; it takes hard work, effort, and sometimes professional help.) My financial situation hadn't changed, and my life still seemed to be falling apart. My two cars were still about to be repossessed. Four of our seven properties were still behind on the mortgage payments. However, the more I affirmed my identity statement, the more I believed it. The more I believed it, the more it changed how I responded to my current situation. Finally, I began to understand that my identity was who I was apart from what I did and from what I had. After my salvation experience, this was the first step in becoming unstoppable.

Even though I had discovered my identity, nothing in my circumstances changed right away. It was a process that took time. Yet something was vastly different inside. I felt a calmness and confidence that everything was going to be okay. Instead of being overwhelmed with hopelessness, I felt deep peace within. I don't know how I knew, but I was certain that everything was going to change. Knowing my identity in Christ gave me confidence and security.

"The Bourne Identity"

Scripture talks about each of us having a "flesh" nature, which is also referred to as the "old self." It is our natural tendency to fulfill our own desires. However, when we accept Jesus Christ as Lord, we receive a new nature referred to as the "new self," and a desire is awakened within us to pursue what God desires. Ephesians tells believers they must "put off the old self and put on the new self." This means we have some choices to make in the process. How do we do that?

I know it might sound somewhat confusing at first, but have you ever seen the movie *The Bourne Identity*? The lead character was known as Jason Bourne, but that was not his given name. In his secretive work for the government, he had willingly trained himself so deeply in his new identity that it became who he was; it superseded his birth identity. Amnesia caused him to forget he even had another name. In the same way, we should become so immersed in who God says we are, and the mission He has for us, that we completely forget the way we were without Him.

God's Word has numerous promises regarding this new identity or exchanged life. For example, instead of having a righteousness based in works, which is like filthy rags (Isaiah 64:6), you have been made the righteousness of God in Christ Jesus, clothed in His glory (2 Corinthians 5:21). Instead of being alone and without hope, God promises never to leave us nor forsake us (Deuteronomy 31:8). We have unending hope in Him. These are just samples of the promises God has for you when you accept Christ. By God's great design, these truths are meant to transform your heart from feeling guilt, pain, and shame, to recognizing that you are free, forgiven, and accepted.

Identity Stealers

Once you know who you are, you have to stay on guard against identity stealers. Identity theft can be

DISCOVERING YOUR IDENTITY

so sneaky. It happens when you start finding your sense of confidence and value in other things. You can't let your success define you, and you can't let your failure define you, either. While it's true that our circumstances play a role in developing who we are, God will use what's going on around you to develop what's inside of you. However, He won't let it define you.

We see this with Peter, one of the twelve disciples of Jesus. On the night before Jesus was crucified on the cross, Peter was sitting around a campfire outside the temple. He was asked if he knew Jesus, but Peter denied ever knowing Him—not once, not twice, but three times. Earlier that night, Jesus had told Peter that he would deny Him, and Peter boldly proclaimed, "Even if I have to die with you, I will never disown you" (Matthew 26:35). Peter blew his chance to prove his love and faithfulness to Jesus; however, even though he failed this time, he later became a catalyst of transformation by boldly preaching the gospel and eventually by giving his life as a martyr for Jesus.

The circumstances you go through build and reveal your character. However, circumstances never define you. God wants you to see what He sees. He made you, and only He can truly define you.

Another identity stealer is affirmation, especially from social media. Nowadays, it's easy to live for other people's affirmation. We post our most flattering photos, best vacation moments, and pictures that show our love for family and friends, even if we were just griping them out right before the picture was taken! Come on, parents, I know that I am not the only one who has done that. I mean, who posts their worst day? Not me. I don't post my bad-hair days. I don't post a picture of my belly when I am struggling with "dun-lap" disease. (You know what I'm talking about? Dunlap disease is where your belly dun-laps over your belt.) Nope, you post selfies in the gym to show the progress of your hard work, all the while hoping others will affirm and admire how good you're looking. Often, as you look at other people's fitness journeys on social media, you start to compare yourself with them. And it's rare that you feel better about yourselves, so you begin to build a fake persona and a fake life, and you never get out of the rat race.

We subconsciously live for the approval of others and begin to morph into someone we are not. Why? Because people will "love" and "like" and "heart" your fakeness and validate the pretender you've become. It makes you feel good about yourself and think, *Well, people like me, I must be doing something right.* The question, though, isn't if people like you; the question is: do you know who you are, and are you living your life according to God's design and purpose for your life?

If you are not careful, you will live your life as a counterfeit. Your life will be fake because you will not be true to the real you. Instead, you will be living to please others and gain their acceptance.

If you don't know who you are, you allow people and circumstances to define who you are. That's why you can have what others perceive as a good life and still feel empty, unfulfilled, and powerless.

If You Don't Know Who You Are, You Will Never Know Who You Are Not

Holding on to my true identity means making choices based on who I am and not on what's happening in my circumstances. That's why when I was broke and about to lose everything after the restaurant shut down, Phyllis and I chose not to file for bankruptcy. I knew that it was a legal option available to me. However, I didn't file for bankruptcy because something within me rose up and said, "Generals don't file for bankruptcy." Generals keep pressing on and marching forward. Generals say, "With God's help, I can do this. I've got this."

> The question isn't if people like you; the question is: Do you know who you are, and are you living your life according to God's design and purpose for your life?

Please know that I am not against filing for bankruptcy, nor am I saying that it is wrong. I am just telling you what I felt was the right choice for me. I felt like this was a test. At the time, I didn't realize this one decision would take me a decade to live out. It took me ten years to pay off all the debt, but with God's help, Phyllis and I did it. Yes, it took us a long time, but guess what? This general made it through, and now I've learned how to better steward money. I've learned that even if it takes a long time, God will give me the strength and grace to walk through the process.

As I reflect on my life, I realize the experience of uncovering my identity was more powerful than I knew at the time. I now have the advantage of more than eighteen years of living with the revelation of who God created me to be. Nothing and no one can hold you back or keep you down when you know who you are and you stay submitted and surrendered to God's will for your life. There is nothing and nobody that can stop *God's plan* for your life. Nobody!

Identity Establishes Your Real Value

If you are like me, you probably don't spend much time thinking about whether the money in your wallet is real or counterfeit. I used to think that counterfeiting money was a thing of the past. However, I was wrong. According to the United States Department of the Treasury, an estimated $70 million in counterfeit bills are in circulation today! That's approximately one counterfeit note for every ten thousand in genuine currency. It's a big problem, and solving it is the responsibility of U.S. Secret Service agents who safeguard America's financial and payment systems from criminal exploitation.

As part of their extensive hands-on training to detect counterfeit currency, the agents spend time studying real money. They examine the way it looks, the way it smells, the way it feels. They familiarize themselves with genuine currency so that when they encounter a bill that's not real, they know it! Here's what's interesting: Those of us who do not study money may receive counterfeit currency and never even realize it. To us, it all looks the same and feels the same. It makes me wonder: How many Christians are living counterfeit lives and don't even know it? They are living the life that others have told them to live, and it's being passed off as the real thing.

Only you and God know the difference. You know because something feels off. Sure, affirmation feels good. Sure, success feels good, but it's just never enough to fully satisfy you. That's because those things are not meant to define you. If your value is found in what you do, you are living a counterfeit life. However, if you know who you are and live authentically, you won't need other people to affirm you and give you value because your identity comes from God himself.

The Test of "No"

Over the years, my identity has often been tested. Many times I felt overlooked and undervalued. In fact, God has never allowed people to validate me the way I wanted to be validated. Looking back, I see that it's not because He doesn't care for me; it's actually the opposite. He loves me so much that He doesn't want me to embrace a counterfeit identity. He wants to make sure my value doesn't come from people's validation; it comes from Him alone.

I had only been on the job a couple of months when I asked my boss if I could speak at a training session I was preparing. It was a session to equip leaders on the mission field, and I knew I could teach the content effectively and memorably. After all, I was the one writing the content, so I thought my boss would readily agree to my request. I will never forget what happened next. My boss looked me in the eyes and said, "Jimn, I didn't hire you to speak; I hired you to organize events and write." My heart sank as I heard those words in our weekly one-on-one meeting. She went on to clarify that public speaking was not currently in my future. My job was to write the content and ensure our communicators had what they needed to effectively teach and train our leaders for the mission field. That's it—nothing more, nothing less.

I sat there in shock and disbelief, looking like a deer caught in the headlights. I was unable to speak or respond. It was hard to breathe. I felt like a ton of bricks on my chest had crushed my dream. All I could do was nod and try not to let my boss see my great disappointment. It was then that I realized for the first time that her expectations and my expectations were not the same. Questions began to flood my mind. *What just happened? What have I gotten myself into? Have I made the right move coming to this organization? Did my wife and I uproot our entire lives to move to a place that will never unlock what I believe God has placed inside of me?*

Only three months earlier, while riding in a boat on the Amazon River, this same person had asked me if I would be interested in applying for this position. At the time, Phyllis and I were in Peru, leading a group of teenagers on a mission trip for the organization. It was there that my boss heard me speak, and I was confident that she enjoyed it. I would often see her smile and affirm me while communicating with the teenagers on the trip. So, after accepting the job, I just assumed that God would open opportunities for me to speak and develop my gift. But you know what they say, assumption is the lowest form of knowledge. In hindsight, if I had known what I had just learned from my boss, I wouldn't have made a move.

Looking back, I had to trust that God let this detail slip because He was ordering my steps anyway. Yet here I was, only months on a new job, and now this door was slammed shut. It felt like I had the rug pulled right out from underneath me. *Did I make a mistake? Did I uproot my family and miss you, God?* I was convinced my boss had missed God's intent. She clearly didn't hear from Him or she would have valued my gift of communication. At that point, as far as I was concerned, she and the ministry were both lucky to have me there. To not have me speak was a real mistake on their part, according to my prideful thinking.

I left that meeting and went back to my cubicle. I thought, *This isn't fair. I can't believe she doesn't appreciate me. I should just quit and go back home.* I was upset, but then something shifted inside me. I turned on some worship music and began to pray and cry out to God. In my moment of despair, I began to feel the presence of God and He spoke to my heart, "I've got you." Then God brought my attention to the story of David, whom God anointed as king, while he was faithfully tending to his father's sheep (1 Samuel 16). Even though his family had overlooked him, God didn't. God knew right where to find David when he was ready.

At that moment I remembered my identity statement and who God said that I was. It was like God was reminding me, "Jimn, remember who you are . . . who I called you to be. Even when you don't feel like it, that's who you are." I decided then that if I never spoke again, I would give my best to writing. If I couldn't speak like a general, then I would write like a general. That's who I was, and nothing could change that. Regardless of what I was asked to do, I would do it the way a general would do it—like I was training and equipping an army. I poured my heart and soul into every manual I wrote, every event I organized, and every session I created. I decided that I made the task; the task did not make me. I was determined to learn and develop myself and my skills, so that no matter what God called me to do, I would be ready, just like David was out in the field.

Five months later, after this test to see if I would fully surrender my life even when I didn't understand or agree, my boss's boss came in and said, "Jimn, I want you to speak." My boss was there and said, "No, he's organizing the event." Her boss said, "That's great. But I still need him to speak for me because I'm not going to be there." He turned to me and said, "Jimn, I want you to take my notes and speak on my behalf."

I was shocked at his request but quickly said, "Yes. I'll do my very best." He said, "I know you will." I took his notes and poured my heart and soul into preparing for this opportunity. I practiced for twenty-plus hours to deliver a forty-minute session. I practiced as if I were speaking to thousands of people, even though I knew there would only be about fifty people in attendance. I went all in. I practiced communicating my stories and punch lines. I worked on crafting the perfect welcome and smooth transitions. Finally, the day came for me to deliver the session. When I got up to the platform to speak, I looked in the back of the room and there was my boss's boss. He hadn't left town after all. Teaching this session was a test. He wanted to see how well I would prepare and communicate the content—especially if I thought he wouldn't be there. I was grateful I had spent the time practicing and preparing. At times, I had been tempted to cut my preparation short. The previous week had been unusually busy and I could have easily made an excuse, but something inside me told me to make sure to do my very best. Thankfully, my preparation paid off.

Shortly afterward, I was promoted to the emcee of the entire ministry. I would end up speaking to thousands of people in hundreds of environments, both live and filmed. The next four years of my life would be a great season of preparation, growth, and impact. It was nothing I could have made happen on my own. The only thing I did was choose to be faithful with what God had placed in my hand. I don't say these things to impress you, but to impress *upon* you that God can and will promote you when it's time. If you know your identity, if you know who you are in Christ, then you won't get offended when someone tells you no. Neither people nor your circumstances give you your value; God does. He knows your name and He knows your location. That's the power of identity.

The God Standard

Imagine that I have a one-hundred-dollar bill in my hand. If I ask you what it's worth, what would you say? If you could identify the number on it, you would say "one hundred dollars," right? If you couldn't identify what I had in my hand, you wouldn't know its value. But here's what's interesting, the one-hundred-dollar bill is just a piece of paper. Aside from the design, the only difference between the piece of paper and a one-hundred-dollar bill is what it's backed by. A one-hundred-dollar bill is backed by gold, and a regular piece of paper is not.

Until 1971, our paper money was backed up in reserve by the government with real gold. It's what was called the gold standard. If I had a one-hundred-dollar bill, there was actual gold sitting somewhere

DISCOVERING YOUR IDENTITY

that guaranteed the value of the paper that I had in my hand. That's what gave printed money its real value. Without the gold standard, it was simply a piece of paper.

Let me ask you: if I offered you a one-hundred-dollar bill, would you want it? What if I tore it or crumpled it up in my hand . . . would you still want it? Would you want a tattered and torn one-hundred-dollar bill? What if I threw it on the ground and stepped on it? Would you want a beat-down, stepped-on one-hundred-dollar bill? Of course you would! As long as the one-hundred-dollar bill is authentic, its value doesn't change, no matter what happens to it. It doesn't matter who steps on it, whether it's been spat on, used, or tattered and torn, it's still worth the same. Just like that one-hundred-dollar bill, no matter what you go through in life, you will never lose your value either. You are way more valuable than any bill that the federal reserve can print. As a child of God, you have a secure backing. Your value is not based on your current condition or status in life. Your value comes from what your life is backed up by: God. Your identity in Christ is not just backed up by the gold standard. It is backed by the God standard!

If you've never really considered your value based on your identity in Christ, I want you to stop and think about it for a moment. Don't ever allow the opinions of others to make you think less of yourself and devalue you, push you to the side, or step on you. I love what Eleanor Roosevelt said: "No one can make you feel inferior without your consent." Maybe life has been harsh. Maybe you feel tattered and torn. That doesn't change your value in God's eyes and should not in yours. You are still the same person. You are who God calls you to be, even when others can't see what He's placed inside of you.

The only way for you to understand your real value is to discover who you are in Christ. When you discover your true identity, nobody can make you feel "less than." No person, no situation can diminish your worth. A genuine one-hundred-dollar bill has value whether someone believes it or not. Someone else's belief does not change the fact that it's legal tender. If someone throws it in the trash, it still has value. Some of you feel discarded in life, pushed to the side, stepped on, torn up, and devalued. Let me tell you today: it doesn't matter what someone else did to you. It may not have been right or fair, but it doesn't change your value. It doesn't change your identity, and it doesn't change what God has in store for your future. It's time for you to recognize your worth because when you know who God made you to be, it doesn't matter what anyone else says or does.

David understood this when he declared, "I am fearfully and wonderfully made" (Psalm 139:14). Where you are doesn't determine your value. Whose you are does.

Let's look at what Paul says in 2 Corinthians 11:23-28 (NLT). He had been through a lot. There's no way anyone could experience what Paul went through without understanding their identity. He says, "I have worked harder, been put in prison more often, been whipped times without number, and faced death again and again. Five different times the Jewish leaders gave me thirty-nine lashes. Three times I was beaten with rods. Once I was stoned. Three times I was shipwrecked. Once I spent a whole night and a day adrift at sea. I have traveled on many long journeys. I have faced danger from rivers and from robbers. I have faced danger from my own people, the Jews, as well as from the Gentiles. I have faced danger in the cities, in the deserts, and on the seas. And I have faced danger for men who claim to be believers but are not. I have worked hard and long, enduring many sleepless nights. I have been hungry and thirsty and have often gone without food. I have shivered in the cold, without enough clothing to keep me warm. Then, besides all of this, I have the daily burden of my concern for all the churches."

And we think we have problems! You may have experienced some of the same sufferings that Paul describes, but he faced them all—and his main concern was for the churches! How could he keep moving forward despite all those obstacles? It's because he knew who he was in Christ and what he was called to do. No matter what struggle, no matter what challenge, no matter what obstacle he faced, he was not going to waver in his God-given identity or resolve, and because of that, he was unstoppable.

Identity in Christ Breaks the Chains of the Past

Failure, whether real or perceived, brings with it chains that, unless dealt with, will hold you back and limit your life. Remember the baby elephant I talked about earlier who failed to break free from the chains of his captor and lived a life of confinement even though he had the strength to be free. The trauma of failure caused him to lose his identity and to live a life of captivity. His will was broken, he was defeated in his mind, and he no longer saw himself as the mighty animal that he truly was. He didn't know his identity. If that elephant knew who he was and the power he had, he would no longer be held captive.

In the same way, when you know your identity in Christ as revealed in God's Word, when you know the power you have available to you through Christ, the chains of the past that have held you back will be broken. You will realize that regardless of the failure you've experienced, your identity is not that of a failure but that of a champion in Christ. Failure is an experience, not an identity. We all try things and fail, but experiences don't define us. Failure is an opportunity for growth. It's not the opposite of success. It's part of the journey to success.

When you don't know your identity in Christ, it's easy to lose yourself in the pain of the past. You will begin to lose your sense of who you really are. I know I did. I allowed the events of my life to limit who I was and what I could do. I no longer saw what God saw and couldn't do what He created me to do. I felt like a failure and became paralyzed by fear. But when you know who you are, you see that failure isn't final. You don't fail. You learn. Each time you get knocked down, your identity in Christ helps you get right back up so you can keep moving your life forward—unstuck and unstoppable in Him.

Scan here to download your copy of **Discovering Your Identity** *ebook.*

CHAPTER 8

Living Life With Purpose

Your greatest fear should not be fear of failure but of succeeding at something that really doesn't matter.

—D.L. Moody

The next building block to becoming unstoppable is understanding your purpose. Once you discover who you are, then it's time to discover what God wants you to do. God created you for a purpose, and it's your responsibility to discover what that purpose is and then fulfill it. Can you imagine having a smartphone and the only thing you ever use on the phone is the calculator app? What a waste of potential. The same is true for you and me. We are filled with untapped potential, and we have to learn what that potential is and how to fulfill it. That's the definition of true success: discovering and fulfilling God's purpose for your life. Nothing more and nothing less.

Your purpose is your assignment. It's what you were designed for. Your purpose is multifaceted. While you have an individual purpose, it will align with God's general purpose for the body of Christ, and ultimately with humanity. Your first and highest purpose is to know God and become more like Him. Jesus told his followers "Love the Lord your God with all your heart and with all your soul and with all your mind" and to "love your neighbor as yourself" (Matthew 22:37, 39). Drawing from those commandments, in his book *Think on These Things: Living with an Eternal Perspective* Ken Boa encourages believers to see their purpose to "love God completely, love myself correctly, and love others compassionately." Certain aspects of living out your God-given purpose such as being an ambassador for Christ (what a privilege as well as responsibility!) do not change. But your temporal purpose may be fluid. It can change and adjust with the seasons of your life. Your earthly assignments, tasks, and responsibilities will change.

My purpose changed as I moved from teenager to young adult, to newly married husband, to father, to pastor, etc. I've worked for different nonprofit organizations, for-profit companies, and churches, ultimately leading our church as the founding senior pastor. Through each season of my life, my earthly purpose was different. Who I am didn't change, but I lived in different cities with different people and different responsibilities. Ultimately, I was still responsible for discovering and living out God's

LIVING LIFE WITH PURPOSE

overall purpose for my life in each season. Even now, though I am pastoring Anchor Bend Church, I am adding and subtracting responsibilities according to God's purpose for my life in this season. For example, I am now not only pastoring, but also writing this book. I felt the Lord lead me to start writing, so now I am living out God's purpose in this new season as a pastor and as an author. And even though there's constant change, my life is still in alignment with my identity as I live out God's purposes.

My pastor, mentor, and friend, Chris Hodges says, "Design reveals destiny." In other words, when you discover how God made you, you can then discover what He wants you to do: your purpose. It's that simple. But the only way to truly discover who you are and what you are supposed to do is through a relationship with your Creator. According to Ephesians 2:10 (AMPC), "For we are God's [own] handiwork (His workmanship), recreated in Christ Jesus, [born anew] that we may do those good works which God predestined (planned beforehand) for us [taking paths which He prepared ahead of time], that we should walk in them [living the good life which He prearranged and made ready for us to live]."

God created you with a purpose and for a purpose.

Getting Back on Track

One time, Phyllis and I were invited to a black-tie event to celebrate our friends' twenty-five years of prison ministry. It was being held at City Center in West Houston at the Hotel Sorella Ballroom. We had just moved into the area, and we were not familiar with this part of the city, so we had to get directions from MapQuest. This was before Google, Waze, Apple Maps—all of them. In fact, I think it was the first digital map widely available. And it wasn't even on a phone. It was a website and you had to print off the directions before you left home. Siri was brand new, and nobody really used it. And boy, we sure felt high tech!

On the night of the event, Phyllis and I were all dressed up and ready to leave. We had just enough time to get to the event without being late. We were excited about our night out on the town with friends as we jumped into our car. At first, all was well. I followed the directions on MapQuest to a T, yet as it showed that we should be arriving at the ballroom, we found ourselves in a neighborhood, surrounded by homes. It didn't seem like we were in the right place. It was pitch black, and clearly no hotel ballroom anywhere in sight.

I asked Phyllis, "Do you think we went the right way?"

She said, "I don't think so."

I said, "But this is what the directions said. I pulled them myself."

Things started to get a little tense between us. We went back and forth a bit and she finally exclaimed, "You said you wanted my help but clearly you don't!" At that point, we started to have a "passionate" discussion. Finally, we came to a stop in front of a house. I was frustrated. She was frustrated. She was stressed out. I was stressed out. We realized we were lost in the middle of a neighborhood and had no idea where to go. Finally, Phyllis suggested we use this brand-new tool on our phones called Siri and see if it would help with directions. I was unfamiliar with Siri and wasn't even sure I trusted it. However, we needed help and were out of other options. I blurted out, "Hey Siri! Give me directions to Hotel Sorella Ballroom." Nothing happened. I thought, "See it doesn't work anyway." I tried again, and nothing. It was then that we realized we did not have cell phone service. Back in the day, we had spotty cell service at best in this part of town. I started driving around and finally got to a place where we had service. Once we got connected, I asked again, "Hey Siri, give me directions to Hotel

Sorella Ballroom." Finally! It worked! We arrived even though our original directions were wrong; we connected to the source who helped us find the way.

Now, suppose you built a roadmap for your life, so to speak, and you thought you had it all planned out. However, after following your plan, you didn't end up where you intended to go. Maybe you climbed the ladder of success and thought you would be happier, but you were miserable just like I was. Maybe you thought your marriage would complete you, but instead of feeling complete you were lonelier than ever. Or maybe you bought your new house or new car and you thought it would make you happy, but then you found yourself feeling depressed, lost, and without a sense of purpose. The only way to get back on track is to get connected to the source who has the roadmap of your life. Since God created you, only He can lead you to the place of fulfillment. He is your source of divine purpose. No matter how lost you may feel, God knows how to get you back on track. You are never lost when you call on Him.

You Can't Bypass the Process

There is a process in discovering and living out your purpose, and truthfully, it does not always happen swiftly.

In 2008, before starting Anchor Bend Church, I moved to Houston to be a part of a campus launch for the church I grew up in. My pastor called me one day and asked if I would be interested in helping him. What's interesting was that at the same time, the organization I was working for had plans to promote me into a position that I could get really excited about. I wouldn't have to travel as much and would be able to lead at the highest level in the organization. So, I had a choice to make. And as if that wasn't enough, the senior pastor of a church in Tyler, Texas, had offered me the opportunity to take over his church. He had plans to move on as a bishop in his denomination and he felt like I was the right guy to take care of the church. I had preached for him several times and helped him with the young adult group at one point. He laid out a two-year transition plan that, at the end, would set me up to be the lead pastor of a fast-growing, multicultural church that he had built. They already owned a multi-million-dollar building located on a great piece of property right off the highway. They were averaging more than 1,000 people every Sunday. To most people, this was the opportunity of a lifetime.

Yet I continued to feel God drawing me to Houston to be a part of the campus launch, even though it made no practical sense. This opportunity was much different from the others. There was no full-time position or sizable salary with benefits to entice me. There were no staff or financial incentives in place to lean on. In fact, if I were to take this position, I would have to get a full-time secular job just to support my family. As crazy as it sounds, I felt the Lord really spoke to me that Houston was our destination, and that if I stayed in Tyler that would be me trying to fulfill God's vision for my life through my own strength. I felt God bring me back to the story in Genesis chapter 16 of Abraham and Sarah. God promised them a son in their old age, and when God didn't seem to be moving fast enough, Sarah gave Abraham her maid to sleep with as a surrogate, resulting in the birth of Ishmael. They tried to birth God's promise through their own power. However, God spoke to Abraham and said that the promise would come through Sarah. Abraham believed and would see God do what He promised. Sarah would eventually birth Isaac, and he would fulfill God's promise to Abraham.

I knew that I had a choice. I could go the direction that seemed right to me: the influence, the money, the title, and the position. It made sense to my natural thinking. It was the right, upward direction, but I knew then that it would be me trying to fulfill God's promise with my power. I told Phyllis what I felt the Lord was speaking to me. She agreed, so off to Houston we went.

The next four years were anything but easy and comfortable. When you are fulfilling your purpose, it doesn't always mean you will like what you're doing. When Jesus was fulfilling His purpose, He pleaded with His Father, "Father, if you are willing, take this cup from me," but then added, "yet not my will, but yours be done" (Luke 22:42). Our comfort is not always a top priority. As I have shared, many times in my life God had me doing something I didn't necessarily enjoy, but He was working on my character or developing a skill in my life that I would need to fulfill something He called me to do in the next season.

Though I knew I was in God's perfect will, I often would find myself wanting to quit and give up, but I didn't. I made a conscious decision that if I did this for the rest of my life, it would be okay because God is worthy of my sacrifice and my best effort. I let go of any expectation or time frame I previously held onto. I had something greater in me that I believed God was calling me to. I knew who I was and what I was supposed to be doing, but this was different. It was His vision for my life that kept me moving forward through the pain. "For it is God who works in you to will and to act in order to fulfill his good purpose"

(Philippians 2:13). If God is allowing something to happen to you, then that means He wants to do something in you.

Embrace the Process

God is more concerned about your character than He is about your comfort. We need to remember that. He's a good Father. Earthly parents who love their kids don't always seek the easy route for them; it's more important to build character in them. Sometimes character development is tough. It's hard. It's doing what you don't want to do so that you become the man or woman that you've always wanted to be.

Imagine a kid saying, "Hey, Mom, Dad, we want to skip school." They may even make a good argument. My kids are no exception. Their smartphones have a calculator that provides all the math they need. If they have any history questions, all they need to do is ask Siri. At school, the teacher tells them things they don't want to learn, and holds them accountable. School is hard, and it takes discipline to study and learn new complex ideas. It takes effort. Yet as a parent or guardian, our job is to make sure they grow into responsible, disciplined, educated adults.

In the same way, God is focused on our personal development. He wants His children to love Him, love their families, and focus on building His kingdom. Since God is a good God, He's going to allow us to walk through some difficult circumstances that will cultivate character within us and develop us into the men and women that He wants us to be.

That's why James tell us, "Consider it pure joy, my brothers and sisters, whenever you face trials of many kinds, because you know that the testing of your faith produces perseverance" (James 1:2). How could James tell us to consider our trials *pure joy*? Because even though life is tough, he knows what happens on the other side. Sure, it's difficult now, but God is at work in your life. People are watching, and we can't live as Christ if the only thing we want is what's easy. We have to be willing to go through tough situations and embrace God's process. Don't be surprised that your faith in God will cost you. I love what John Maxwell says: "A faith that has not been tested is a faith that cannot be trusted." Let's make a decision that no matter what we go through, whether it's easy or it's hard, we choose to trust God. And as we do, our joy comes from Him, not our circumstances.

Carry the Weight for Which You Were Designed

Identity and purpose go hand in hand. If you don't know who you are, it's easy to find yourself doing what God never intended for you to do. It's not uncommon for people to get pulled out of God's purpose for their lives because of the pressure and expectation of others. Psychologists call someone who allows identity and the direction of life to be defined by others' influences a "dependent" person—someone who is not differentiated (knowing who they are, apart from others). Living a "dependent" life results in a lack of accomplishments, low self-esteem, being easily swayed by others, and underperforming in all aspects of life.

In my travels over the years, one of the many things that has always fascinated me is how people in different countries use motorbikes and motor scooters for transportation. It seems everywhere you go, motorbikes are used by the masses. Now, the original intent of these motorbikes is for personal use. They are designed to hold one or two people, maybe three at most. However, in certain countries overseas, it is not unusual to see an entire family to load onto a motor scooter! Or, in lieu of a truck or trailer, you may see these bikes piled high with five feet of stuff! It's a miracle someone can even ride it this way. But here's what I know, the motorbike may not break down immediately, but eventually the bike will break down under the weight of a load it was never created to carry.

The same is true for you and me. How many people do you know who have been crushed under the weight of being overloaded? If we aren't clear on our God-given purpose, it can become difficult to say no to people. Saying no stems from the confidence in knowing who you are in Christ and what you're supposed to be doing . . . or not doing. I heard a statement that sums it all up, "If you'll learn to say no, you'll trade popularity for respect."[10]

Being overloaded isn't just about activity. It's also about emotional burdens. You aren't meant to carry worry, fear, or regret. What happens when we say yes and carry things we shouldn't? Whether it's an activity or an emotional burden, we get overwhelmed, and ultimately, we can become angry and bitter. We know deep down inside we are doing too much.

> If you'll learn to say no, you'll trade popularity for respect.
>
> —GREG MCKEOWN

For example, there are people walking around today who are frustrated and essentially "broken down" on the side of the road of life. They got stuck because they were overloaded. They were carrying more than they were designed to carry. Now they are angry, frustrated, or living in hurt. And here's the reality: if that's you today, it's your responsibility to say no. It's time to shake off that heavy burden, leave it on the side of the road, and get back up and on with fulfilling the destiny God has for you.

Keep Your Purpose in Perspective within the Bigger Picture

Your story, your purpose, is part of a bigger picture in which the body of Christ works together for a common purpose. We are in this together. The Bible says that just as the human body has many parts—an eye, an ear, or a leg—so the body of Christ also has many parts (1 Corinthians 12:12-31.) Each part has a specific function or purpose to fulfill. You were created by God. You are not an accident. He made you on purpose for a purpose. *The Message* says it like this:

> *You can easily enough see how this kind of thing works by looking no further than your own body. Your body has many parts—limbs, organs, cells—but no*

matter how many parts you can name, you're still one body. It's the same with Christ. The way God designed our bodies is a model for understanding our lives together as a church: every part dependent on every other part, the parts we mention and the parts we don't, the parts we see and the parts we don't. If one part hurts, every other part is involved in the hurt, and in the healing. If one part flourishes, every other part enters into the exuberance. You are Christ's body—that's who you are! You must never forget this. Only as you accept your part of that body does your "part" mean anything. You're familiar with some of the parts that God has formed in his church, which is His "body." (1 Corinthians 12:12, 25-27, MSG)

Don't be an ear trying to carry the weight of a leg just because you think a leg looks good and you want to be a leg. Understand that legs carry weight that an ear was never intended to carry. Imagine if an ear were to try to hold that weight of a body because it wanted to be a leg. What would happen? It would be crushed. Why? Because it is not designed to carry that kind of weight. But it doesn't mean an ear doesn't have great value. It does, and it carries weight in its own way. Its value is in hearing what's happening outside of the body. Although the weight isn't physical, there is a weight or heaviness of listening. When we understand our part and role in the whole body, we see how each part is vitally important. No position carries more importance than any other in the body of Christ.

Ultimately, God wants to bless you in the purpose He's called you to. Remember, as a Father, He delights in His children and delights in those who serve Him. His heart is that you would find joy in your purpose and come alive inspiring others. I love how Howard Thurman put it, "Don't ask what the world needs. Ask what makes you come alive and go do it. Because what the world needs is people who have come alive."

Your Purpose Is Eternal

The book of Jeremiah opens with God speaking to him: "Before I formed you in the womb I knew you, before you were born I set you apart; I appointed you a prophet to the nations" (Jeremiah 1:5). Jeremiah lived during Old Testament times and had specific revelation regarding his purpose. And just as God assigned Jeremiah a purpose before he was born, God also had a purpose in creating you. Ephesians 1:4 says this: "For He chose us in him before the creation of the world." And 1 Peter 2:9 tells us that we are a chosen people, called to declare the praises of the One who has called us out of darkness into His marvelous light. You have an assignment from God, and once you discover it and begin to live it out, it will bring fulfillment and joy to your life.

Scan here to watch my message, **"Living Life With Purpose***."*

CHAPTER 9

Moving Your Life Forward With Vision

*Vision is the spectacular that
inspires us to carry out the mundane.*

—Chris Widener

Once you know who you are and what your purpose is in the current season, you need to develop a vision for where you're going. Vision is the ability to see beyond your present reality into the future reality God has for you. It's seeing what's beyond the now. If God is the source of vision, then your vision should be an extension of His vision for your life. You and I are a small part of something greater. We fit into the master plan God has for each life, the world, and the universe. God is working in you, giving you the desire and the power to do what pleases Him (Philippians 2:13). He is the one who can help you see beyond your current reality. His vision for you is not just about your job or ministry, but embraces every area of your life such as your marriage, family, finances, health, spiritual life, morality, etc. God wants you to have vision in every area of your life. It's the picture of what can be. It's the limitless possibility of your future with God as He directs your every step.

Vision is the passion and fuel for life. It's what keeps you going when the going gets tough. It's what helps you realize that where you are is not where you will end up. Your current situation or struggle is just a place that you are passing through. The Psalmist said it so well in Psalm 23 when he said, "Even though I walk through the darkest valley, I will fear no evil." Notice he says, "walk through the valley." Vision moves us forward in life and keeps us from camping out in the valley of disappointment and despair. Without vision, you will end up getting stuck, camping out in the middle of your mess. You'll end up dead or dying.

From Genesis to Revelation, God makes sure His people have a vision of His plan. Tragically, humanity often does not follow it, but God has revealed His plan. Ancient wisdom from the book of Proverbs puts it this way: "Where there is no vision [no revelation of God and His word], the people are unrestrained; But happy and blessed is he who keeps the law [of God]" (29:18 AMP). Another version says, "Where there is no vision, the people perish" (KJV). Does this mean physical death? Or is it something else? Maybe internal, relational, or emotional death? The answer is yes. It can be any or all of the above. Without vision, a person has nothing rewarding, nothing beyond the day to live for, whether physically, emotionally, or relationally. Life is empty and void. It is simply existing, drifting from one place to the next, aimlessly searching for meaning within the monotony of the mundane or temporary pleasure of life, some of which lead you to where I was: on drugs. God never intended for you to merely exist. His plan is to for you to live fully alive and moving forward each day with His vision out in front of you.

You Become What You See

"If I had the chance to do it all again, I wouldn't do it. It's the worst decision I ever made." My grandfather was describing the lap-band surgery he had years ago to help him lose weight. He had first tried many other diet fads and weight-loss programs, but nothing seemed to work. He would lose a few pounds here or there, but eventually, he would put it back on, so he decided that he would have the lap-band surgery. He had heard stories of people who lost weight and kept the weight off long-term. He did his research, and after much deliberating, he decided this was the course of action he needed to ensure a long and healthy life. The idea behind the procedure is that if you can't physically eat as much, you can't gain weight. And it works for some people. But there are many others—some studies show as many as seventy percent—who have had lap-band surgery who do not manage to lose any significant amount of weight. They eat just like they used to eat until their stomach and intestines stretch back out, so nothing changes. My grandfather was one of them. He is just as heavy today as he was when he had the surgery—if not more—and I've always wondered why that was.

Fast forward to a couple of years ago. I was in Montana with a group of pastors and was complimenting one of them on his recent weight loss. I had known him for a couple of years, and it was amazing to see his transformation. He had dropped more than 150 pounds and was looking great. I asked him how he did it, and he went on to tell me his story.

He told me he had lap-band surgery, and much like my grandpa, it didn't work. He was frustrated and angry at the lack of results. However, his failure to lose weight led him on a journey where he discovered that the success of weight loss isn't really about what surgery you have—it's about your self-image.

I was curious and asked him to explain. He went on to tell me that his journey led him to a doctor who agreed to perform a gastric sleeve surgery on him, with one caveat. Before doing the procedure, the doctor required my friend to commit to several months of intense counseling: it was non-negotiable. The purpose of the counseling wasn't to address his physical weight; it was to address his emotional weight. This doctor knew that if he would focus on losing the weight in his soul, he would do better with the surgery to lose the weight on his body.

The counseling helped him realize that he had a self-image problem, not a weight problem. Even though he had lap-band surgery, he failed to see the results he wanted because he was subconsciously sabotaging his progress. With the help of his counselor, he was able to reimagine himself and develop a new vision of who he wanted to become. After that, he no longer thought of himself as fat or overweight, a person without self-control, but instead he saw himself as a person of discipline, healthy and strong. That was the secret to his ultimate transformation and weight loss. Because he developed a clear vision of who he wanted to become, he was able to reimagine himself by first changing his thoughts about himself, and then over time, he changed his life.

Maybe you are reading this and you don't know God's vision for your life. Or maybe you do, and you've just lost sight of it or placed it on the shelf, so to speak. Either way, the enemy is constantly working hard to keep you from seeing God's vision for your life. He knows that if you can't see your future, you'll never experience it. You can only build in your life what you first see in your life. Maybe, unknowingly, you allowed your thoughts to focus on the wrong things. You let yourself go on autopilot. Thoughts filled your mind like, "Man, I can't believe I don't have enough money for retirement. I'm going to have to work until I'm seventy." "My kids are never going to leave home." "I am always going to be overweight." "I'll never be disciplined enough to read my Bible every day." Whenever you have such negative thoughts, you imagine the worst-case scenario for your future. You are reinforcing a negative image of your future and ultimately bringing into reality the vision you see. Without the right vision, you'll get frustrated, discouraged, and hopeless when hard times come. That's what happens when your current struggles are all you can see.

Everyone needs a vision for the future. The challenge is when you focus so much on your present circumstances that you can't see beyond where you are now. You've been in your mess for so long, it's all you can see. And if the mess is all you can see, then you'll stay stuck. So what do you do? Dig into what God's Word says about His will and His sustaining power, and ask God to give you a fresh vision. Ask Him to help you see what you can't see. You might feel like you are in the middle of the battle, down in the trenches. But God is not. He sees beyond this battle. He may be waiting for you to ask Him to help you discover vision and purpose for your life.

What I've learned is that I need something greater than my problems to live for—something that pulls me through my day of pain and keeps me moving forward so that when a bad day comes, I've got something pulling me out. As I mentioned before, Psalm 23 says, "Even though I walk through the darkest valley..." The phrase "walk through" is key here. You are not meant to camp out in the valley of the shadow of death. You have to see yourself moving through to the other side. You have to keep your eyes looking up. You always go in the direction of your vision.

So maybe you're in debt. The question is, can you see yourself debt-free? If your marriage is on the rocks, can you see your marriage being healthy? Can you visualize you and your spouse having the best decade of your life, growing older and closer together? Can you envision a godly family that is functioning with love and respect—not dysfunctional, but healthy? Can you envision your life moving forward, not being emotionally stuck in fear, depression, and anxiety? Can you imagine yourself being happy and full of joy—not perfect, but healthy? Can you imagine yourself in a better place than where you are right now? If not, it's time to get a vision.

Write down what you want for the future. Find some applicable Scriptures that tell you what God says about your circumstances. Jesus promised that those who abide in His Word are His disciples, and His disciples would know the truth and the truth would make them free (John 8:31-32). Meditate on God's Word until His truths become what you see, what you expect. Just like my pastor friend who lost 150 pounds, it may take a while to retrain your vision in light of your circumstances, but don't give up. Time is moving on anyway, so you might as well use that time to reshape your future in ways consistent with God's Word.

See the Potential, Not the Problems

In 2020, we began purchasing our new church campus in Richmond, Texas, and we were so thrilled. I remember taking our leadership team and our trustees to go and look at the building for the first time. It was as if everyone had the same thought: "God, are you sure this is the location you want us to move the church to? Are you sure you want this to be our new location?" The building was in rough condition. The structure was solid, but it had been neglected for years and would require a lot of work before we could meet there for church. The parking lot was too small, the roof was leaking, the electrical and plumbing fixtures were outdated. At the time, we had a decision to make. We could see all the problems and work before us, or we could see the potential opportunity of what God brought our way. I love what Thomas Edison said, "Opportunity is missed by most people because it is dressed in overalls and looks like work." God allowed us to see the potential, not the problems.

Some people only see the problems. And guess what—if all you are looking for is problems, you will likely get more problems. That vision can dramatically affect your future.

We don't want problems to direct our future; we want God's vision to direct our future. For example, we hired an architectural firm to help us develop a vision for our new campus. We wanted everyone to see where we were headed, so we had the architect draw blueprints to get a picture of the future for our new building. We then developed a plan on how to get there.

Vision helps us stay on track. Without a vision for the property, it would have been easy to get frustrated with the construction process. Construction is messy. When things get tough, you need a vision for what's ahead so you don't quit and give up throughout the process.

Similarly, when you have God's vision for your personal life, you are not worried when you find yourself in the middle of a construction phase. Just as a construction site is messy, our lives, when under God's construction, are messy too. It's God's vision for our lives that helps us see that God is not done with us. Instead, He is working and remodeling and renovating our lives into a masterpiece (Ephesians 2:10).

> Opportunity is missed by most people because it is dressed in overalls and looks like work.
> —THOMAS EDISON

Again, on the personal side, the devil wants you

MOVING YOUR LIFE FORWARD WITH VISION

to feel like you've been sidetracked and derailed throughout God's construction process. He wants you to believe the mess you are in is all that you will ever be. He wants you to lose hope and quit God's construction process so you never become the masterpiece God has designed for your life. Just know that the devil is a liar and the father of lies (John 8:44). If you hear his voice in your head saying things like, "You will never amount to anything," "You've messed up too badly," or "God doesn't care about you," refuse to believe his lies and choose to trust that God is walking you through the process of healing and restoration. Grab hold of Philippians 1:6, which says, "Being confident of this, that he who began a good work in you will carry it on to completion until the day of Christ Jesus." God loves you and has a vision for your life. Nothing is ever lost or wasted with Him. He can catapult you to where you need to be.

Our God is the God of the impossible (Jeremiah 32:27). You are not in this alone; you have the God factor. The God factor says, "Anything is possible to those who believe" (Mark 9:23). Choose to believe what God says about you and the plans He has laid in your heart. The devil doesn't win unless you quit. Choose right now that you are not quitting! Say this with me now: "I cannot quit, I will not quit, quitting is not an option." Choose to receive God's vision for your future. Let Him tear down the old and build something new in you. Trust Him through the process. If you are reading this and feel like your life is in ruins, know that the Master Builder has the blueprints. Getting through the demo phase is part of the process. My prayer for you is from Ephesians 1:18: "I pray that the eyes of your heart may be enlightened in order that you may know the hope to which he has called you."

Vision Produces Endurance

One day I was scrolling through the television channels and stumbled across a documentary about Noah. I found it fascinating, and I was geeking out on the history. However, I stopped to think about the fact that Noah stayed focused on one word from God for over a hundred years! Pause to think about that. He believed God and locked onto that vision for his future like a hungry dog with a bone. There was nothing that was going to deter him from his purpose or from doing what God said. One moment of revelation fueled his resolve for an entire century. Nowadays, it seems like we need confirmation and assurance every day! Oh, to have the faith and resolve of Noah. His clear vision for the future produced endurance in him to accomplish what God assigned him to do.

Vision will keep you pressing on when life gets tough, when you are tired, frustrated, and ready to quit. When you get discouraged and feel hopeless, God's vision for your life will carry you through until the end. I love this quote by Chris Widener: "Vision is the spectacular that inspires us to carry out the mundane."

Faithful in the Field

God is working in you now to prepare you for what's ahead, and your job is to work with Him during the process. As humans, we tend to long for something greater, but tragically, few will do what it takes to prepare for what God has in store. That preparation may include patience.

Sometimes we are so focused on the greater thing that's in our future that we forget to notice what God has for us right now. Don't let the future promise pull you out of your current work. It is critical to understand that God is using you now, where you are today, on the way to where you are going. Don't despise the day of small things (Zechariah 4:10).

Remember the story of my boss telling me I wasn't going to be a speaker? If I had gotten offended and decided to make my own way, I would have missed what God was working out in me behind the scenes. I had to trust that God had a purpose for me right where I was, even when I didn't understand or agree on the route God was taking to get me to what I saw for my future.

Even while David was out in the field tending to the sheep, he knew where he was headed. He'd had a vision of where God was taking him after Samuel anointed him to be king. David was headed to the palace; however, he never stopped fulfilling his purpose in the field. He knew his future calling and the greatness God placed within him, yet he remained in the field tending his father's sheep until the time was right. It was in the field where the king's servant found David and extended an invitation for him to play the harp before King Saul. David was in the field when Jesse, his father, called on him to take food to his brothers on the battlefield where Goliath and the Philistines were mocking the people of God. It looked like David was faithfully running an errand for his dad, but really, he was on an assignment for God to go slay a giant. This is why Scripture tells us to be faithful in the little things. Imagine if David had told his father, "I'm not taking food to my brothers. I've been anointed to be the next king. They should be bringing me food." With that attitude, David would have missed the very thing that catapulted him into his destiny.

I want to encourage you today: While you need vision for your future, don't be so focused on it that you miss what God is doing to prepare you today. Don't see yourself as "too good" for the little things because by being faithful in the little things, you put yourself in a position for God to make you ruler over much. It's the little things that nobody else wants to do, the little things that aren't impressive, the little things that bring no accolades and no title; these little things might be the very assignment from God that unlocks your destiny and the vision God gave you. Don't get ahead of God by trying to make things happen on your own. You'll only succeed in accomplishing God's vision for your life when you do it His way and in His timing.

Scan here to watch my message,
"Moving Your Life Forward With Vision."

CHAPTER 10

The Power of Paradigms

*Often, people live trapped in a cage of their own
making, and they are simply unaware of it.*

Once you discover your identity and purpose, and you have a vision for your future, it's time to evaluate your paradigms. Remember, as previously defined, a paradigm is "a way of seeing based on implicit or explicit rules that shape one's perspective." It's your conscious and subconscious pattern or habit of thought. We have both conscious and subconscious paradigms that provide a framework for the way we view life. To get unstuck and move forward, we need to explore both paradigms and their power over our lives for good or bad.

For example, suppose that when you were young, you were in a car that was hit by a semi-truck. As a result, you may always have an uneasy feeling when driving past semi-trucks. You may not even remember the event, but that experience could powerfully affect your subconscious paradigm. A neural pathway was created in your brain that sealed an association between semi-trucks and trauma/danger. The belief that all semi-trucks are dangerous becomes a part of your subconscious paradigm, and this idea runs in the background of your mind without conscious thought. It affects how you drive, whether you are consciously aware of it or not.

Neurobiologists and cognitive psychologists say up to ninety-five percent of your behavior is habitual. Therefore, your subconscious paradigm controls most what you do; it's your habitual, automated behavior, and most people never realize this is happening unless they stop and think about it, analyze it, and become consciously aware of it. Have you ever done something and then thought, *Why did I do that? What was I thinking?* Your subconscious programming or paradigm was the catalyst for your behavior even though you were not aware of it.

Subconscious paradigms are built over your lifetime by the environment you grew up in and the people you were raised with. They are also formed through your life experiences. Your subconscious paradigm is the single most significant influence on your decisions, the friends you have, the lifestyle you live, the habits you form, and ultimately the life you live. Our goal as believers is to align our paradigms (both conscious and subconscious) with God's Word, so that the way we view the world is in alignment with the way God views the world.

We live in a fallen world, raised by imperfect people, so it's safe to say we all have dysfunction in our paradigms. The good news is that you can change your paradigm and reprogram your subconscious. As Romans 12:2 tells us, "Do not conform to the pattern of this world, but be transformed by the renewing of your mind. Then you will be able to test and approve what God's will is—his good, pleasing and perfect will." We are to renew our minds with the Word of God. It's only through His Word that you will be able to leave behind your old worldly or ungodly paradigms and find yourself right in the middle of His good, acceptable, and perfect will!

Sabotaged from Within

Self-sabotage is more common than you think. Often, people live trapped in a cage of their own making, and they are simply unaware of it. They are living on autopilot, driven by their subconscious paradigm. Their lives are producing the negative results that their ungodly paradigm has been programmed to produce. Sure, they desire more. They have a vision for the future; they know it's possible, but something seems to be holding them back.

When we self-sabotage, we become stuck in a cycle of bad choices, sinful habits, and repeated failures. Some of the core beliefs of self-sabotage are "I'm not enough;" "I don't deserve better because of things I've done or who I am;" "I'm not as smart, talented, rich, or educated as others;" and "I grew up on the wrong side of the tracks." We subconsciously tell ourselves these lies based on our experiences in life. Whether true or false, when we believe these thoughts, they become our paradigm, the lens of our perceived reality. But just because you think something doesn't mean it's true. Second Corinthians 10:5-6 says it like this, "We use our powerful God-tools for smashing warped philosophies, tearing down barriers erected against the truth of God, fitting every loose thought and emotion and impulse into the structure of life shaped by Christ" (MSG). We need to form our paradigm around the truth of God's Word, which never changes.

A Picture of How the Subconscious Works

To understand paradigm, we must first get a basic understanding of how our conscious and subconscious minds work. Think of your conscious mind like a gardener. "Seeds" are planted in the form of ideas in the field of your thought life. This happens in your conscious mind. You are aware of what you are thinking. Your subconscious mind is like the soil of the field where the seeds are planted. It's where the seeds (ideas) germinate and grow and produce whatever you've sown. Just like a seed in the earth is growing even when you can't see it, your subconscious mind is working day and night to cultivate the seeds in your mind to make your behavior fit the pattern of your thoughts, ideas, hopes, and dreams. Simply put, your subconscious mind grows whatever is planted. Whether trees or weeds, whichever seed your conscious mind sows is what is produced in your life. Your subconscious mind is powerful. It makes everything you say and do fit a pattern consistent with your paradigm.

Another way to think about this process is the way an app works on your phone. Your conscious mind is like the screen on your smartphone, and your subconscious mind is like an app running in the background with your unconscious mind as the operating system. It's not visible on the screen, but it is running programming and constantly sending messages to the home screen.

Our family uses an app called Life 360. It's a great app designed for family and friends to see where everyone is and ensure they are safe. Phyllis and I have two teenage boys, both with phones. We all have the app, and we love it because we all know where we all are at all times. As we travel from place to place, the app sends us notifications of where everyone is and when we have arrived safely. I regularly get notifications from the app while I'm working to let me know that "Caden has arrived at school" or "Carson has arrived at a friend's house." Based on the message I receive, I respond accordingly. Each message has the ability to impact and alter what I'm doing in a moment's notice.

Don't think this app is just for parents to spy on kids; it works the other way, too. A while back, I was working at the office and having a really rough day, so I decided I needed a break. I decided to play hooky. Yes, like a delinquent teenager, I just left the office. I was like, "I got to go." And I left. I didn't think anything of it. I forgot all about the app. I was enjoying a few relaxing moments at an undisclosed location when I got a text from my son, Caden. This was unusual, especially since it was right in the middle of the school day. Caden rarely texts me unless he needs something or unless something is wrong.

So immediately I texted back, "What's going on, son? What's happening? Is everything all right?" He said, "Yes, dad. Everything's good."

I said, "Are you in school?"

"I'm in school."

"Are you alive?"

"Yes."

"Are you breathing?"

"Yes."

"You got all your fingers and toes?"

"Yes, yes. Yes. Yes."

"Great. Well, then why are you texting me?"

He said, "Well, Dad, I'm texting you because I wanted to know why you are at the movies." I froze in my seat—I was so busted! He had received a message saying, "Dad has safely arrived at Cinemark Movie Theater." I sat there for a moment to gather my thoughts and then texted back, "It's research, Caden, research … don't tell your mama." Though my response was lighthearted, the movie was already ruined. I felt guilty and ashamed, like I had done something wrong, even though I hadn't. Feelings of inadequacy and insecurity flooded my mind. *How could I take a break? What was I thinking? I need to work harder and muscle through.* The thoughts were endless. I ended up leaving the movie theater and going back to work. It was just like that app running in the background. Ultimately, my paradigm caused me to miss out on a moment of rest and decompression that was healthy and okay.

Think about what happens when you get ready to take a test in school, or you want to ask a girl out, or you are trying to lose weight, or you want to start a business. Does something inside say, "You're not good enough" or "You're a failure"? If so, that's bad programming from your subconscious. That's your paradigm needing to be adjusted. Somewhere along the way, a lie was implanted into your subconscious mind, and without realizing it, it caused you to make certain choices in your life that maybe you don't even understand.

Your Paradigms Shape Your Reality

Your paradigms shape the way you interpret what you experience. It's what explains how two people can have a shared experience and yet come away with two completely different realities of what just happened. Even though they share the same experience, they have different subconscious paradigms or filters, which produces two very different realities of what happened.

A simple way to illustrate this is with a glass that is filled halfway with water. It's not full or empty. The water level is right in the middle. When you look at that glass, what do you see? How would you refer to the glass? There are two basic responses. Some would see the glass as half full, while others might see it as half empty. Who's right? Both are right. Both perspectives are valid and could be summed up as true statements. It's your reality.

Why is that important? Does it matter? Yes, because what you see determines the way you respond. If you see the glass as half full, you will be mentally and emotionally more content and subconsciously more satisfied. For example, if you're out eating a meal with friends and you see that your water glass is half full, then subconsciously you're going to enjoy your meal and enjoy the people you are with because you don't see yourself as needing anything else to drink. However, if you see the glass as half empty, you'll be mentally and emotionally more discontent. You will subconsciously be dissatisfied with your current state of being. Without much conscious thought, you will begin to respond with anxiety. Thoughts will flood your mind like, "I need more water. Where's the waiter? When are they coming back to refill my glass?" You may even disrupt the contentment of others at the table and ask them to help you to look for the waiter so that you don't run out of water. You are reacting to the situation because of what you see when you look at the half-filled glass.

I know this is a simple illustration, but it helps you get an idea of how unaware we can be of our subconscious programming and how even something as simple as how we view a glass of water impacts our lives. It's not what happens to you, but how you interpret what happens to you that matters most.

Paradigms Control Habitual Behavior

We've talked about how a paradigm can be likened to an unseen app that has been installed in your subconscious mind. It is constantly running in the background of your life and has almost exclusive control over your habitual behavior.

Remember, up to ninety-five percent of your behavior is habitual. The way you eat is a habit. You don't have to sit down and think about how to chew food, do you? Even decisions like what you eat and when you eat are affected a lot by your paradigms. Paradigms control the way you think. They determine your reason and logic. Have you ever had someone say, "Well, that's illogical? That's impossible." What is that? That's their paradigm being expressed in a thought that goes outside of their programming. Paradigms can impact everything from creativity to productivity—what gets done and how it gets done. Even the way you manage time is a byproduct of your paradigm. Your paradigms create the reality that you live in.

God Changes Paul's Paradigm

Going back to the apostle Paul, we know that his life was radically changed after he encountered Jesus on the road to Damascus. We can see his transformation through what he wrote in the New Testament. His words have been a guide for Christians for thousands of years and have helped many to experience change in their own lives.

What you may not know is that after Paul's conversion, he went immediately into the desert of Arabia for three years. During that time the Holy Spirit began a deep work in him which continued throughout his life-long ministry of communicating divine truth as he spoke and wrote letters to the early church. We see this transformation as we read his writings in the New Testament.

What happened during those three years was only the beginning of a lifelong process where God would change Paul's thought patterns and transform him into the image of Christ. Even though he was born again, he still had to allow God to transform his old paradigm. His mentality and mindset was then shifted from a temporal perspective to a true eternal perspective. Before his conversion, Paul was as religious as anyone. He was a radical zealot (Gal 1:14; Acts 22:3). Though he was religious, it wasn't until he had an encounter with Jesus on the road to Damascus that his life was forever changed through relationship with Him.

Religion leads us to rules and legalism, but relationship leads to life change and transformation. We can see Paul's transformation through his writings as he encourages and challenges us throughout Scripture. Paul wrote more than half of the New Testament. His writings are a clear indication of the deep inner transformation of his heart.

In his letter to the Philippian church, he writes, "Let this mind be in you, which was also in Christ Jesus" (Philippians 2:5 KJV). What does that mean? In

THE POWER OF PARADIGMS

this sentence, the word "mind" in the original Greek indicates habit of thought expressed by deeds.

What he's saying is, "Let the habit of thought in you be the same that was in Christ Jesus." So, whatever Jesus's habit of thought was should also be your habit of thought. This tells us we need to examine the way we think. We need to take time to consider and reflect on what fills our minds, conscious and subconscious. Then we need to work to make sure our thoughts align with the same thoughts that filled Christ Jesus.

When I was younger, I read this passage and worked hard on my conscious thoughts; however, I neglected the subconscious. To be candid, I never considered or even thought about my subconscious mind. I neglected it simply out of ignorance. At the time, I didn't know anything about the subconscious mind. It wouldn't be until many years later that I began counseling and realized there is a part of me on the inside that I never realized existed. It's like standing on an iceberg and never realizing that what I can see is only a fraction of what is really there. Most of the iceberg is under the surface of the water.

Building A New Highway

When Paul wrote, "Do not conform to the pattern of

this world" (Romans 12:2), what pattern do you think he was talking about? That's your old habit of thought, or paradigms. "Don't conform to the paradigms of this world." But look, he says, "Be transformed." Transformation involves metamorphosis. You were one thing, but now God is making you into a brand new thing.

A great example of this is the transformation of a caterpillar to a butterfly. The butterfly starts as a caterpillar that undergoes a transformation. Something happens to the caterpillar after it has spun itself into its chrysalis. The caterpillar exchanges its old nature for a completely new one. It becomes complete mush and loses form in the darkness. But then something far more beautiful appears. It really is remarkable!

These truths are captured in a video I saw online by Elevation Church called, *The Human Brain:*[11]

· The human brain is made of approximately one hundred billion neurons.
· That's approximately the number of stars that exist within our galaxy.
· The human brain monitors and regulates all of the body's actions and reactions.

- With over five trillion chemical operations occurring every second, and signals being transferred at speeds of over 260 miles per hour, our brain rapidly analyzes and responds to all the sights, sounds, and smells all around us.

- Because we are all born slaves to sin, our minds have been programmed to behave out of selfish desire.

- The way we think, dream, reason, and act are limited to the ways of this world.

- For every behavior you experience, your brain creates a neurological pathway.

- As behaviors are repeated, those pathways become increasingly more stable.

- Think of it this way: a single behavior maps on a dirt road in your brain, creating a basic pathway for your thoughts to travel.

- As you repeat behaviors, your brain builds a highway, allowing for an increased volume and frequency of thoughts to move about, resulting in your day-to-day actions.

- In order to change our behavior, we must reprogram our brains, a process that takes time due to deconstruction of existing highways.

- The Bible directs us to take every thought captive and to commit daily to the renewing of our minds through the power of God's Word, and in time the result is the formation of an entirely new neurological roadmap, leading you to the life you were meant to live.

Transformation requires the deconstruction of old existing highways or patterns of thoughts and the building of new neurological pathways that align with God's Word. It's about aligning yourself, your thoughts, your will, your purpose to His. Living a life for Him is not about just being saved so you can make it to heaven; it's bigger than that. It's letting God transform you here on earth, and that's a lifelong process. If you don't understand this process, it can cause great frustration in your life.

You have to be committed to a lifelong journey and realize not everything can be fixed instantly or in a matter of weeks, months, or even years. Healing comes in layers. It takes time. Transformation happens in stages. God continually works on us. And the problem is that people try to shorten the process or bypass it altogether. But you can't. You have to work through the pain in order to experience the promise. Why? Because God's working in you. He wants to change ungodly paradigms that were caused by pain and trauma of the past that you didn't even know were still sabotaging your life. Look at what the prophet Jeremiah said: "The heart is more deceitful than all else and is desperately sick. Who can understand it?" (Jeremiah 17:9) God knows what's hidden in the layers of your subconscious, and if you'll submit to His process, He will show you the hidden pain and trauma that formed ungodly paradigms, finally bringing healing to your life.

You may not feel like your life is worth much now. You might feel like a pile of mush inside a dark, lonely cocoon. But the Spirit of God hovers over the dark places in our lives. When the power of God gets inside you, He will transform you from the inside out and make you something far more beautiful than you could have ever imagined. You're not the same in any way, shape, or form. It all happens as you renew your mind to the Word of God.

How do we experience transformation? The answer is in the same verse. It's "By the renewing of your mind." The word "renewing" actually means remodel or reconstruction. If you've ever done a home remodel or construction project, you know that before you can bring in anything new to the space, you have to do some demolition. You have to knock some things out, and it gets messy.

The same is true for us. A lot of times people get mad at God when things get messy. Sometimes things get messy because the devil is trying to do the demolition, so to speak, but even when the devil is the one trying to destroy things, let me tell you, he's not going to have the last word. The devil may try to come in and do some demolition, but God is going to come back in and rebuild.

When things get messy, remember God is building something new in your life!

Scan here to watch my message, **"The Power of Paradigms."**

CHAPTER 11

Getting to the Root: How Paradigms Are Formed

You can attempt to change behavior, but without addressing the root, the change will not last.

The last chapter described how paradigms are formed through ideas planted in your subconscious mind, but let's dig a little deeper and get to the root. It's important to note that when the Bible talks about what we know today as the subconscious, it addresses it as the "heart" of the person, or the person's innermost being. This is what it means when it says: "Above all else, guard your heart, for everything you do flows from it" (Proverbs 4:23). Everything you do flows from your heart . . . from your subconscious paradigms.

Think about that for a moment. You have a place deep inside you that houses beliefs and "programs" running your life, that most people are unaware of. That's why you have to guard your heart intentionally. The way you do that is by protecting the gates of your heart: your eyes, your ears, your words, and your thoughts. The problem is that while we are young, we don't have control over what we see, hear, and experience, so thoughts and ideas are planted into our subconscious (heart) without our awareness. They are planted into your subconscious mind in two primary ways: environmental conditioning and heightened emotional experiences.

Environmental Conditioning

Environmental conditioning is when ideas are planted into your subconscious mind by repetition of exposure. No one understands this more than marketers. They know that if they can repeatedly expose you to their messages, those messages will take root and eventually you are likely to buy what the marketers are selling. What you expose yourself to matters. What you watch matters. What you listen to matters. Who you spend time with matters. The apostle Paul speaks to this when he says, "Bad company corrupts good character" (1 Corinthians 15:33).

Your environment and the people you are around shape and form you. It's those experiences and the thoughts and ideas that stem from those experiences that become the program that runs your life. In fact, the factor that has the greatest impact on your paradigms is the environment you experienced as a child. Some people grew up in a home environment where their parents worked together to create a healthy home life. But he or she may have experienced a teacher or coach who spoke words of failure, discouragement, or doubt. Some people had a difficult upbringing in which there was abuse, neglect, and eventual brokenness. However, they had adult influences that provided hope and encouragement that helped heal those broken paradigms. The truth is that we live in a fallen world, and everyone experiences its effect at some point in life.

Children are like sponges that soak up the environment around them without any effort. They are constantly absorbing what people around them say and do. As a child, you develop all of your likes and dislikes, your beliefs, and social norms as your conscious and subconscious paradigms are formed. The music you listen to, the way you vote, the food you eat, and the car you drive are impacted by the way your childhood experiences formed your views on life.

For example, I drive a Ford truck, and my affinity for Ford trucks started as a teenager. I worked for a man named Joe that I admired when I was seventeen years old. He owned a successful lawn business, and one day while we were out cutting grass with his crew, I made a comment about liking a Chevy truck that passed by. He laughed out loud and said, "I would never buy a Chevy truck." His comment caught me off-guard. The truck that had driven by was decked out and looked impressive. I didn't drive a truck at the time, nor did anyone in my family. I really didn't have an opinion on which brand of truck I thought was best. So, I asked Joe, "Why not? Why don't you like Chevy trucks?" He said, "A Chevy's not a truck; it's just a toy." (To all the Chevy truck owners reading this book, it's not personal!) But then he added, "Any truck that has to put the words W/T on the side to say it's a work truck is no truck at all. That's why I drive a Ford truck."

At the time, I didn't realize the power of his words in my life. Unknowingly, that idea about Chevy trucks was so firmly planted in my seventeen-year-old mind that when I bought my first truck at forty years old, guess what kind of truck I bought? Yep, a Ford pickup truck, without even thinking about it. I didn't even realize why I chose a Ford until I began this journey of understanding paradigms.

All of us have ideas like this that have been planted into our subconscious minds and have formed a master program for our lives over the years. When you're a child, you're being programmed. You're learning and growing and soaking up your environment, good or bad. It's all going straight into your subconscious, and without even realizing it, when you're an adult, you have this programming running in the background of your life.

Heightened Emotional Experiences

The second way your subconscious mind is programmed is through heightened emotional experiences, including any experience that intensifies your emotions more than normal. It plants a thought in your mind that, if believed, becomes seared into your paradigm. It can be either a positive or a negative experience. A *positive* heightened emotional experience is an event like the birth of a child, a proposal, or a financial windfall. Maybe you were a wide receiver on your high school football team and caught a pass that scored a winning touchdown during the last thirty seconds of the fourth quarter of the state championship game. Maybe your spouse threw you a surprise fortieth birthday party. Such intensely joyful experiences usually produce positive thoughts that, if believed, become a part of your subconscious paradigm.

Similarly, a heightened *negative* emotional experience produces pessimistic thoughts that, if believed, become a part of your subconscious paradigm. Thus, that negativity will become a permanent part of your conscious and subconscious paradigm and will begin to sabotage your life by producing negative thoughts and negative behaviors in your life.

Behavior Modification

If you try to change your behavior without addressing your underlying paradigms, your subconscious may sabotage your attempt to change. You may experience temporary change, but without addressing the root of the behavior, change will not last. The results amount to nothing more than behavioral modification. As long as you have a system or program to stay connected to, your behavior changes. For example, a person who is trying to lose weight and working with a personal trainer is successful whenever he or she has that personal accountability and support. However, the moment the person gets out of that supportive environment, he or she will slip back into the old way of life. Have you been there?

Slipping back happens spiritually as well; it's what some Christians call "backsliding." For example, when I was young, I would go to church, and as long as I was actively involved in serving or in a small group, my life moved forward spiritually. However, if anything disrupted my supportive environment, I would fall back into my old sinful behaviors based on my old way of thinking or my old paradigms.

Many people get stuck in a never-ending cycle because they fail to address their old paradigms. That's why it's important to "throw off your old sinful nature and your former way of life, which is corrupted by lust and deception. Instead, let the Spirit renew your thoughts and attitudes" (Ephesians 4:22-23 NLT). Not only should you "throw off" your old nature, but also you have to "make new" your thoughts and attitudes. In other words, there has to be a transformation of your old way of thinking and your old paradigms. It takes more than putting yourself in an environment with accountability and sound teaching for this to happen.

To experience lasting behavior change requires both a supportive environment and a safe place to address underlying paradigms. Otherwise, you end up with nothing more than behavioral modification and not heart transformation. This is why people who try to lose weight fail in their attempts time and time again. It's why addicts who have been sober for years relapse after losing their support system. It's why young adults who attend a multi-year transformative internship or college can go back to their old way of life within a couple of years after graduating.

I watched this reality play out while I was on staff at a national youth ministry. Over twenty years, this nonprofit organization enrolled thousands of high school graduates and college students in its internship program for one, two, three, or even four years. The program was an intense "spiritual boot camp." Its focus was to develop leaders and shape each participant into an active, engaged, fully committed follower of Christ. While some students were successful at maintaining the gains made through the training, many were not. Over the years, I have run into students who appeared to thrive during their internship; however, they had become angry and bitter afterward. They shared with me their frustration with the ministry, former leaders, and saddest of all, with themselves. Their goal of developing a transformed life that would facilitate a dream of changing the world for God was short-lived once they left the ministry. Most of them gave it their best while at the ministry and appeared to thrive while going to character-development classes, participating in fasting retreats, running in a 5K, doing corporate exercises, attending accountability groups, and serving on teams that facilitated ministry that literally impacted the world. And yet none of that was enough. Sadly, for many, their excitement and growth didn't continue once they left. The staff, who were the architects of this program, had falsely presumed that simply pulling students out of their normal environment and placing them into a supercharged, high-intensity, high-impact spiritual environment for one to four years would produce change that would last. It has been heartbreaking to see the negative impact this program had on so many lives.

At first, I dismissed most complaints as something being wrong with the individuals. I would point them back to reconcile with those who had hurt and wounded them. After all, I was not only a staff member, but I was also actively engaged in this training myself, and it had a positive impact on me. In fact, I loved every minute of what I did during my time at this ministry. I would say that this ministry changed my life and helped me become the man I am today. However, I have since come to realize that those students are not to carry the full weight of this failure alone. I am not minimizing their responsibility for change, but I now realize the power of the subconscious. I understand that unless it is addressed and changed, it can sabotage one's entire life. Again, my heart breaks to see the guilt, the shame, and the embarrassment of failure that some of these students still carry within themselves today. They've believed the lies of the enemy that they are not good enough or that something is wrong with them, or that they are a failure. Some have even abandoned their faith and are no longer serving God or even going to church.

When I look at why change didn't last, it's almost always because the support system of change was no longer in place to support them. When they left the program and went to a new place, many would experience a culture shock. When all their positive activities were discontinued, there was nothing to maintain their life change. Behavioral modification will never be enough to create lasting change because the problem is internal, not external.

Ultimately, for lasting change to occur in your life, behavioral change must have a support system (church, small group, friends, family, mentors, etc.), and you must address old paradigms. When you overlook this simple but powerful truth, you will fail to experience the lasting change you desire.

Living Out Your Self-Image

I have experienced the struggle with weight loss firsthand as I've worked hard over the years to be a healthy person. I have developed a lifestyle of eating healthily (occasionally indulging in brownies and ice cream—my weakness) and working out. However, when I was growing up, this was not always the case. Early in my teenage years, the idea that I was "fat" was planted deep into my subconscious by something my older brother said in the middle of an argument. It happened one day when my parents were at work, and we got into an intense verbal argument. To this day, I can't remember what the fight was about, but I'll never forget what was said. In the heat of the moment, for whatever reason, my brother said, "It's because you're FAT!" He went on to expound on the idea.

At the time, I was no bigger than a normal adolescent teenager. I was certainly not grossly overweight. However, when he called me fat, a seed was planted in my heart and subconscious that took root in the soil of my heart and became part of my subconscious paradigm. I didn't even realize it when it happened. I shrugged off his comment and acted like it didn't matter; I acted like I was tough and like his words couldn't hurt me. However, as an insecure teenager experiencing the awkwardness of adolescence, his words deeply impacted me and were seared on my subconscious. When he spoke those words, I believed what he said. From then on, I looked at myself differently and began to question what I saw in the mirror. I no longer saw the real me; I saw a fat guy. It didn't matter what numbers were on the scale; it was about the distorted self-image in my heart. The real Jimn began to fade away from that moment on. I saw myself as overweight, even though when I look at pictures of myself now, that simply wasn't true.

It's hard to believe how long my insecurity lasted because of the words spoken by a loved one in the heat of a single moment. I don't think my brother consciously thought, "I am going to say something now that will make my brother struggle with weight his whole life." No, we were just immature teens being stupid. He wouldn't have done anything like that intentionally, but the enemy would. The devil loves to plant lies into our hearts and twist the words of people we love. He wants to steal, kill, and to destroy. I thank God that Jesus has come to provide us with a much more abundant life (John 10:10).

The words you speak not only shape your reality but have the potential to shape the reality of others. Maybe that's why Jesus said, "On the day of judgment people will give account for every careless word they speak" (Matthew 12:36 ESV). He knew the power of words and how they can either bring life or death (Proverbs 18:21). Words are the building blocks of life. They are powerful and should be used wisely.

Maybe as you are reading this now, you're remembering something that was said to you in your early years, or you're remembering an experience that impacted the way you view life. This I know: God wants to heal the wounds and transform your paradigm. Revealing is the beginning of healing. When you go into those broken places, pray and take Jesus with you. Ask Him to shine light in the dark and heal every past wound.

Before that conflict with my older brother, I never thought of myself as being fat. But after that, the struggle was real. No matter how hard I tried to eat right and work out, I could never become fit enough, skinny enough, or healthy enough to erase the fat image from my mind. And yes, it was in my mind, not on my body. I didn't have a weight issue; I had an image issue. I would later come to learn that in order to change the way I looked, I had to change the way I looked at myself—I had to change my paradigm so I could live out a healthy self-image.

Not Good Enough

My twin brother Steve and I played baseball for the local little league when we were in middle school. During one of our games, two opposing ideas were planted into my subconscious. The first one took root after I hit a grand slam: "You're a champion! You're coordinated! You're good at sports!" However, immediately afterward I realized my father wasn't at that game to support me, and the second idea was planted: "You're worthless. You don't have much value."

I didn't realize what was happening then, but I do now. The devil was planting lies into my heart that he would use to try and sabotage my life. It was during this game in a heightened emotional state that I began to believe the lie of the enemy. I would struggle most of my life with feeling not good enough because of the thoughts the enemy planted in my heart. At this game, I had both a positive heightened emotional experience and a negative heightened emotional experience at the same time. Both emotional experiences became a part of my subconscious programing that's been running in the background of my life ever since.

Even earlier in my life, negative seeds had been planted. When I started pre-K, my teacher came in and told the class to write our names. So, I wrote my name the best I could, and I was really excited about it. But when I showed the teacher, she appeared frustrated and said, "I can't believe it. You didn't even try to write your name correctly. I'm going to talk to your mom about this when she comes to pick you up." I immediately thought, Oh my, I don't want to get in trouble. Do you know what I did? I lied. I said it was because of the desk I'm writing on. I had lots of little scratches on it, and caused me to be messy. I don't believe the teacher meant to scar or hurt me. It was just a careless comment, but the damage had been done. An idea was already planted in my subconscious that my best was not good enough. Here I was. I was just a child, and a lie from the enemy was planted in my heart. Remember, ideas that are believed are seeds that are planted in your subconscious.

I don't know about you, but I want to uncover every ungodly paradigm that has been seeded into my conscious and subconscious mind to sabotage my life from within. I'm tired of blaming the devil. I'm tired of blaming people. I'm tired of saying it's you . . . it's this . . . it's that. The reality is, it's me and my internal programming! But the good news is that we have a tool through the Word of God to reprogram that ungodly thinking. I refuse to stay stuck, and I hope you do, too.

Fishing with Johnny

One time when I was fifteen years old, my mom let me spend the night at my friend Johnny's house. She didn't often let us go stay the night with people who didn't go to church, but she did this time. Johnny's dad had a big white boat, and I was thinking, *Praise God, I'll get to go fishing.* Back then, I always wanted to go fishing, but my dad worked all the time, so no one ever took us. This opportunity was a big deal to me. Not only could I go fishing, but I was going fishing on a big, beautiful boat. Friday night I went over to his house. We started to go out on the boat, but it started raining. Well, I was raised in church, so I started to pray, "God, please stop the rain." But the rain didn't stop.

Later that evening, Johnny told me, "Well, if it doesn't rain tomorrow, we'll go fishing then." I thought there was no way my parents would let me stay overnight at Johnny's house. He didn't go to church, and my parents didn't know his parents. Still, I thought I should at least ask to see if I could. I called my mom and, to my surprise, she said yes. That alone was a miracle. So I prayed, "God, please, please don't let it rain. If You love me, please do this one for me. I will never ask You for anything again." I was just fifteen, but I'd heard my whole life that God answers your prayers—not just the big things, but the little things as well. I'd been taught that God loves us and cares about us, and I wanted to hold Him to it. For some reason, this prayer request was a really big deal in my heart.

We got up the next morning and the weather didn't look good, but there was a ray of hope. Even though the clouds were dark, it hadn't started raining. I'll never forget that moment. We started getting on the boat and loading all our stuff, but just as we were getting ready to head out, it started pouring. I cried out to God in my heart, "God, please!" But, the rain didn't stop.

What I didn't realize in that moment of disappointment was that I made an inner vow. It was then that I decided to never again get my hopes up. I just told myself it didn't matter, that I didn't care. I determined that if I never got my hopes up, I could never be let down. I was trying to protect myself, but I recognize now that this was the moment in life where I began to shut down emotionally.

The false notion that "God does miracles, but He doesn't do them for me" was planted into my heart. If God didn't care, then I wouldn't care either. And if I didn't care, I could never be hurt or disappointed again. Subconsciously, from that moment on, I began to control everything that mattered in my life that was within my power to control because I couldn't trust anyone, especially God.

I was shocked when I discovered this lie that had been planted deep in my heart almost thirty years ago. After all, I am a pastor and I have seen God do some incredible things throughout my life. In fact, if you were to tell me about God and his miracle-working power, I would have agreed with you. I would have quoted Scriptures to prove that I agreed with you; however, it was only a surface-level agreement. God's truth was yet to be fully unlocked in my heart. Looking back, I wonder how many opportunities I missed because I didn't realize to what extent my subconscious paradigms were sabotaging my life.

Fast forward to 2019. As the pastor of a portable church, we were presented with the opportunity to purchase the building I described in Chapter Nine. The only problem was, we didn't have the money needed to buy the building. Though our church was financially strong, and we had reserves in the bank, our expansion funds were depleted because we had just completed the remodeling of our Dream Center campus. It was an old Baptist church that we converted into offices with a small auditorium for auxiliary meetings.

If we were going to buy the building, we would have to raise one million dollars in one hundred days. This was going to take a miracle!

After our overseers, trustees, and leadership team spent weeks with financial consultants, we made the decision to pursue the purchase of this building. It would be a step of faith, but we believed God was going to show up in a big way. We believed this building was supposed to be our new church home.

As we started the process, knowing it was going to take a miracle, it wasn't long before I began to have serious doubts and concerns about what we would be able to do. I began to question my leadership, the ability of our people, the economy, and other factors. I didn't know it then, but I see now that I was really wrestling with that false paradigm that "God can do miracles, but not for me." Subconsciously, I believed this miracle was too big for God to do in my life. I knew He could do it for someone else, but I just couldn't believe He would do it for me. I was fully convinced that two of my close friends who were pastors had experienced God's miracle-working power in big ways, not only in their churches but also in buying land and buildings. (Don't think the devil won't use the success of your friends to intensify your pain and dysfunction.) It wasn't long before doubt opened the door to fear and uncertainty in my life, even though much of it was subconscious.

Then one morning I was praying and asking God to speak to me clearly about whether we were supposed to pursue buying the building. With all the risk, I was still uncertain. If I stood up and led our people in this direction, what would happen if God didn't come through? What if we tried and failed? All of the "what ifs" were playing out in my mind, creating a web of confusion. And trust me, I was coming up with plenty of reasons for why we weren't going to be able to do it.

I was desperate and needed an answer. I continued to pray, "God, please just confirm that this is You and not my ego, or me trying to build my kingdom. If it's You, I will go 'all in' regardless of what it might cost me if we fail. *But*, if it's not You, I don't want to do it. Please, just speak clearly to me."

Immediately after that prayer, I opened my prayer journal that I had randomly grabbed earlier that morning. The first Scripture I read at the top of the page was Jeremiah 32:27: "I am the Lord... Is there anything impossible for Me?" I knew it was the Lord lovingly piercing my heart through His Word, addressing all my past trauma, fears, and pains. Tears welled up in my eyes and I felt hope come alive in me that I hadn't felt in years. God's presence and the power of His Word overcame my old ungodly paradigms that were attempting to sabotage my life.

I have come to realize that my question, "God, are we supposed to buy the building?" was not the real question of my heart. I was really asking, "God, can You keep it from raining?" My wounded, teenage self was still asking, "Do You love me enough to do the impossible? I know You do miracles, but will You do them for me?"

Maybe you have a similar question deep down inside. Maybe you're afraid about something. You know God can. You know He will. You know He's done it for others. But you aren't sure if He will do it for you.

When God showed me Jeremiah 32:27 that day, He was reassuring me: "I'm the God of the impossible and I am with you. I've got you. Yes, I can make it rain, and I will, just for you." It took me a while to realize that God was breaking an ungodly paradigm that I believe would have sabotaged the purchase of our brand-new campus. He wants to do the same for you today. He wants to heal every wounded place and turn your past disappointments into reappointments for your future.

Here's the rest of that story. Six months later, in the middle of Covid-19, we purchased that building during a time when most people said it was impossible! God did what only God could do. He used that experience of our church buying the building, a positive emotional experience, to overturn the lies the devil planted deep in my heart and subconscious years ago during a negative heightened emotional experience.

I often think about what would have happened if I hadn't allowed God to reshape my paradigm. Would we have our Richmond campus? Would we be making the impact we are making? Or would I have stayed stuck and subsequently kept our church stuck? It's almost inconceivable that something so small and seemingly insignificant could cause so much pain and potentially sabotage what God wanted to do in our church and in my life.

Maybe you are reading this today, and you have never experienced a major breakthrough like this in your life. Maybe you are at a crossroad. You have an opportunity like I did. You know God is up to something in your life, but you have thoughts like I did: *I can't because … I'll never because …* Don't allow those negative thoughts to sabotage your new season. Remember what God promised Isaiah: "Forget the former things; do not dwell on the past. See, I am doing a new thing!" (Isaiah 43:18-19) But before you can walk into the "new thing" God has for you, you have to have a new paradigm or way of thinking.

I want to encourage you with the words that my friend and mentor, Dino Rizzo, inspired me with, "Don't make God look small." In other words, reform your paradigm to a possibility paradigm. Take the limits off!

Trauma Triggers

Everyone goes through painful moments in life. It might be the death of a loved one, the betrayal of trust by a friend or spouse, or the absence of a mother or father growing up. Sometimes pain is caused by others, and sometimes we cause our own pain through our choices, whether intentional or unintentional. The list of how we experience pain in life is endless. The point is, everyone has experienced things that cause significant pain, and that's what we will refer to as "trauma" (a deeply distressing or disturbing experience), whether you realized it or not. Trauma can occur in a physical context where a bodily injury is inflicted on a person by something or someone externally, or in a psychological context where an emotional injury occurs due to a deeply distressing or disturbing event. Psychological trauma can result from the sudden death of a loved one, an accident, rape, or a natural disaster. As we continue to learn more about subconscious paradigms, we will discuss trauma in a psychological context.[12]

It has been said that time heals all wounds, but that's simply not true. Yes, time is an important factor when it comes to healing. But the reality is, time doesn't heal anything. Time presents you with the opportunity to bury your pain as deeply as you can and avoid it to keep moving forward. This is dangerous because you think you are better off just trying to forget the pain, ignore it, or suppress it, but none of these coping methods are effective long-term solutions. Pain from trauma doesn't just go away; it must be healed. If unhealed, it will manifest in destructive ways in our lives, even if we think there is no correlation.

Time doesn't heal every wound. Many wounds remain, creating ongoing pain that spills over into the lives of those we love and care for most. And, if left unhealed or unresolved, the pain creates trauma in others. Like the old adage warns, "Hurting people hurt people."

Unresolved pain can affect our lives without our even knowing it. It is expressed in moments when that pain is aroused and "trauma triggers" come into play. If someone says or does something that triggers your pain, your response to that person may shoot from zero to a ten in a single moment. You "blow up" or "go off" because that person touches pain that is unresolved. Maybe your boss makes an offhand remark and you light into him or her. Or your spouse or child responds to you in a way that upsets you, and instead of responding in an appropriate way, you blow up. Your response to the situation is extreme: raised voice, yelling, cursing, or saying things that wound the one you love. (FYI, just because you don't raise your voice doesn't mean you are not triggered.) We get triggered when someone says or does something that touches the pain that has been trapped within. Then, when the slightest pressure is felt, you explode.

It's important to note that not all explosive or triggered behavior is solely due to pain. Some of the overreaction can be due to what Randy Powell, my life coach, calls "add ons." These are occasional life stressors that intensify our reactions to a situation. For example, if you have a major project due at work and you come home and "blow up" on your child for something small, it may be because of the current stress at work and not necessarily pain or trauma.

Pain is often suppressed when life gets busy. Healing unresolved pain takes time, energy, and focus. It also often takes a professional to help us process the pain, whether a pastor, psychiatrist, licensed counselor, etc. Sadly, we push aside our pain so often just to keep going in life that we don't realize how much remains unresolved. We live at such a fast pace; it's common to mask the pain and make excuses for its impact in our lives. Instead of working through it, we simply hope it goes away. We may live weeks, months, years, or even a lifetime without realizing something is wrong. In the meantime, we think everyone else is the problem.

It's not uncommon to mistakenly blame the person who causes your "trigger," never realizing the pain is within you. No one can make you do anything. The actions of others cannot make you blow up. No one has power over you unless you give it to them. You're not a victim, yet many people live with a victim mentality. It takes honesty, courage, and vulnerability to admit this. It's always easier to blame others because it validates our pain and keeps us stuck where we're comfortable, which is precisely what the enemy wants. He wants you to remain defensive, paralyzed emotionally, and unable to build healthy relationships with those you love, all the while blaming others and passing on your wounds and trauma.

Pain, if unresolved, begins a vicious cycle of generational bondage. If I hold onto hurt, then I will do what my dad did to me, and then my kids will do to their kids what I did to them. It's time to break generational hurts and be free. Christ died so that we would not live as a hostage to the pain of the past. As a Christian, you are an overcomer, and that means overcoming past trauma through the power of forgiveness (1 John 5:4).

Let me pause here and give you a glimpse into my heart. My intent is not to throw stones or point the finger at anyone. I don't want my words to hurt or wound you. I want them to be the tool that God uses to help you break free and experience healing. I am on a mission to help you. I want to come alongside you, encourage you, and let you know that I have been where you are and I am continuing in this process with you. I wish I could say that I have arrived and never get triggered or blow up, but that's simply not the case. The reason I can write with authority about this is that I have struggled with my own pain and trauma that I continue to work through. I have been in counseling for many years now and continue to see a professional each week.

If you wanted to change your physical condition, you would hire a personal trainer to work with you each week, and it's the same with changing your inner emotional conditioning. Change takes time. Thanks to prayer, intense counseling, forming new habits and disciplines, and a great support system, I am growing and I am healthy, though not perfect. I am still in the process and have to work hard just like you do. I love how Paul said it: "Not that I have already obtained all this, or have already arrived at my goal, but I press on to take hold of that for which Christ Jesus took hold of me" (Philippians 3:12). Let's keep pressing together and do the hard work necessary to experience God's healing.

Scan here to listen to my podcast episode, **"Sabotaged From Within (Subconscious Paradigms)."**

CHAPTER 12

Temptations, Traps, and Hacks

I cannot quit. I will not quit. Quitting is not an option.

It's normal to be tempted to quit throughout this transformative process, but don't you dare! Do you know what you get if you don't change? You get more of what you've already been experiencing: being stuck, miserable, frustrated, and living with regret. In this final chapter, I want to make you aware of some things that will help you stay on course. Remember, true life change doesn't happen overnight. It takes time, effort, and focus. You will face temptations along the way designed to throw you off track. The enemy will try to trap you and convince you to quit. But remember, just because things are not happening on your timetable, it doesn't mean they won't happen.

You must always expect a delay between sowing and reaping, action and reaction. What gets planted in one season is reaped in another. If it were quick and easy, everyone would be able to do it. God's Word encourages us to keep cultivating, planting, and sowing—no matter what things look like in the moment. Paul said it like this: "Let us not become weary in doing good, for at the proper time we will reap a harvest if we do not give up" (Galatians 6:9). For some, the harvest may come sooner than others, but it will come to everyone who holds fast. Know this: Breakthrough is coming.

The One-Yard Line

In February 2021, I was among the 96.4 million other Americans who watched the Super Bowl game between the Tampa Bay Buccaneers and the Kansas City Chiefs. During that game, something happened that I believe is a picture of what you might be experiencing. As the second quarter began, the Chiefs had the ball but were forced to punt after failing to convert on their drive. The Buccaneers, leading 7-3, drove the ball from their thirty-yard line to the Chiefs' one-yard line. All they had to do was move the ball forward one yard to score a touchdown, and they had four plays to do it. But play after play, on all four attempts, they were stopped. They were trying their hardest, but nothing seemed to work. Yet even though they experienced defeat in this failed one-yard attempt, they ultimately went on to win the game 31-9.

Could this be a picture of your life, marriage, family, business, or job? Until now, it seemed like you were moving forward, but recently your progress has been stalled. Nothing you do seems to be working. Maybe you feel like the enemy has stopped you in your tracks, and you are frustrated, angry, or hurt, all because it seemed like you were just about to "score" and now you're stuck.

I want you to know that the devil has mounted an all-out attack against you. Maybe he has blocked your every move. Don't give up. As long as there is breath in your lungs, keep going. Keep pushing, pressing, advancing, and moving forward. The apostle Paul said it like this: "I press on toward the goal to win the prize for which God has called me heavenward in Christ Jesus" (Philippians 3:14). Even if you don't score on this drive, don't give up. As I urged you in the previous chapter, *press on*. Ultimately, we win (Revelation 1:18).

I've learned that all too often, the devil gets too much credit. No doubt, he throws obstacles in your path. But how often do we fail because we just quit? We're on the one-yard line. We get stopped once; we get stopped twice; we get stopped a third time. Maybe we're held scoreless on that drive, and, unlike the Buccaneers, we just give up and forfeit the game.

When we give up too soon, I can sense the devil laughing and saying, "Look, you thought you had your miracle, but my little obstacles were all it took to stop you cold." My prayer is that you break through, push past all the enemy's barriers, and see the fulfillment of God's purpose in your life. Don't quit; you've got this!

"Faith" It 'Til You Make It

But get this. At times you just have to "faith it" 'til you make it. Not fake it, faith it! Sometimes you've just got to put a smile on your face, put on your "leave the house" clothes, and keep moving forward. Some of my most significant breakthroughs occur when I don't feel like anything is happening. In fact, it often feels like just the opposite. It feels like God is distant. I'm praying, but I'm not hearing Him. I'm spending time in His Word, but I'm not feeling Him. I'm struggling. It seems like people are leaving my life and deserting God. I fear that everything is falling apart. And though there are great blessings, there are also intense trials and a sense of, "God, where are You?"

Have you ever felt like that? Have you wondered, *God, where are you?* During such times, I go back to when I was first born again. Do you remember when you first gave your life to Christ? It was like you had a hotline to God. You prayed for your favorite parking spot, and lo and behold, somebody moved out of that spot just as you were driving up. You felt God's presence when you talked to Him. It was like thinking, "God, it'd be nice to have a cool, refreshing diet Dr. Pepper" . . . and somebody walks up and hands you a diet Dr. Pepper. (Just kidding, but it feels like that. It's amazing!)

I believe God does this for a reason: He wants you to feel His love and His connection. But the time comes when we have to grow up. We learn to trust Him and seek His ways—not just His blessings. There comes a point when we have to mature, start eating solid spiritual food, and stop expecting God to baby us. We don't feel everything the way we used to because God is allowing us to grow up and hold fast to our faith. If our walk with Christ was nothing but a warm feeling all the time, we would remain very immature in our spiritual walk.

It's like a parent with a toddler. Dad says, "Come on, baby, you got this. You can walk." His hand holds the toddler's hand, and the toddler feels the strength of dad holding him up. But there comes a point where God lets go of your hand so you can learn to walk on your own. He never leaves or forsakes you (Hebrews 13:5). He's still right there beside you. It's great to feel His presence, but when you don't, you have to take a step of faith. That's the maturing part—knowing my faith walk goes beyond feelings. And what I've realized is that in my life, whenever I don't "feel" God, that's usually a time that my faith is being tested. God is saying, "Will you be faithful in the valley? Will you be faithful in the field? Will you keep on doing what you know to do, whether you feel it or not, whether you like it or not, whether you feel like I'm around or not?" That is maturity.

And I can sense God just saying, "Look at how you're maturing and growing spiritually." God has not abandoned you. He is with you. Don't give up!

Just Go to Bed

Have you ever noticed specific times when you most want to quit? For me, it's usually at night after having a rough day, and anything that could go wrong has gone wrong. Or even worse, at the end of a long week when I am exhausted physically and mentally. I am ready to throw in the towel! I just want to give up. Well, it's during moments like these that I have discovered a simple but powerful solution: I need to go to bed. I have learned that going to bed and getting rest is the best strategy to keep me from quitting or derailing what God wants to do in my life. It's how I cast all my cares on God (1 Peter 5:7). If I were to stay up all night stubbornly trying to fix all my problems, it would be like telling God, "I don't need You." But by choosing to rest, I am relying on God's strength and protection. I love how David said it: "I lie down and sleep; I wake again, because the Lord sustains me" (Psalm 3:5).

Here's my conversation with God on those nights: I say, "Tag, You're it. I'm going to sleep. It's all Yours!" Yep, you read it right. I say all of that, and then I go to sleep. When I give my fatigue and frustrations to God, I can rest in His ability to handle everything. Then, as I rest in God and sleep through the night, my strength is renewed. By the time I wake up and have my quiet time with God in the morning, my perspective has changed. What felt overwhelming and impossible the night before is now possible. I awaken with enough strength for the day. And I only need enough strength for today because it's the only day I can currently live. If I can get through today, I can likewise get through tomorrow. If I can get through tomorrow, I can likewise get through the next day. Half the battle is just getting up rested, one day at a time, and preparing for that day's fight with worship, prayer, and reading God's Word.

Continually Refocus Your Life

Colossians 3:2 says: "Set your minds on things above, not on earthly things." We have to keep refocusing on the thing that really matters: eternity. I'm not going to get distracted with the things of this earth, whether good or bad. The enemy wants us to be distracted. If we get distracted, we will lose focus.

I'm reminded of a story about the 2004 Olympics. An athlete named Matthew Emmons was the best shooter in the three positions, fifteen-meter rifle competition. This guy was a great shot—really, the world's best shooter. He was on the final event and was far ahead of the other competitors before his final shot. He didn't even have to hit a bullseye to win. All he needed to do was hit anywhere on the target, and he would win the gold medal. He lined up the rifle, aimed, he got his breathing and heart rate under control, and pulled the trigger. His bullet hit right in the center of the bullseye. But he lost the competition. When everybody in the crowd gasped, Matthew discovered he had made a bullseye . . . *on the wrong target.* He dropped from first place to last place, all because he got distracted.

If our lives are focused on the wrong things and we don't refocus and check our aim, we will miss the target. It's not just a matter of whether you're moving forward; it's whether you're moving forward *in the right direction.*

Be Unoffendable

Here is another hack to navigating the process: Be unoffendable. I don't think I've ever had more opportunities to be offended than during the ten months of writing this book. We are still living with the reality of Covid-19 and social distancing. Our society has opened back up, but now we are living in two realities. Just about everything nowadays has an option of "in person" or "online." However, with the expansion of life to online or remote, whether work or school, the opportunity for offense seems to be so much greater. Personally, I find that the closer I am to a person relationally, the harder it is for me to be offended by him or her. The closer we are, the more I tend to give grace after an offense. Why? Because the Bible says that love believes the best in others; it covers over a multitude of sins (1 Corinthians 13). Of course, I am talking specifically about being offended by those we know and love, and there are certainly exceptions (such as an affair, betrayal of trust, etc.). But typically, emotional and physical distance are more likely to create distortion.

Jesus taught His disciples that it was impossible to avoid offenses (Luke 17:1). Think about that statement for a moment. How many times did Jesus ever say something was impossible? Not many. But He says it's impossible for offenses not to occur. So, by implication, He is telling us, "Hey, look, get ready, get ready, get ready! Offensive people and situations are going to come your way." Why? Because the devil is trying to separate you from what God has joined you to.

Although Jesus said that offenses are inevitable, He added, "Woe to anyone through whom they come." He challenged His disciples to watch themselves—to refuse to allow the offense to cause damage in their relationships. He then explained what to do when conflicts arise: "If your brother or sister sins against you, rebuke them; and if they repent, forgive them. Even if they sin against you seven times in a day and seven times come back to you saying 'I repent,' you must forgive them" (Luke 17:1-6).

Now, I don't know about you, but if someone is "sinning against me" seven times a day, it might start getting a little more difficult to forgive that person each time. The disciples, knowing how difficult it is to forgive, wisely implore Jesus to "increase our faith."

That's because it takes faith to forgive. It takes faith to believe the best. It takes faith to trust God through a tough situation and choose to forgive, especially when you have every right to feel offended.

Remember, if the devil can get you offended and upset, he can separate you and eventually isolate you. If he can get you offended at your spouse, it creates a barrier between the two of you. Eventually, if you don't forgive each other, you might divorce the very person God joined you with to deal with your unresolved traumas. That's right, your spouse is uniquely equipped to help you heal from the wounds you've carried for years. And yet, if you take offense at something and refuse to forgive, you won't be able to achieve the healing God can provide. The devil wins every time an offense creates separation.

This can happen with your kids, too. Every parent knows how easy it is to be offended when you feel undervalued. Oh, of course, your kids don't know what you've sacrificed to provide for them. They're just kids. But the devil wants to put a seed of offense in your heart. Sometimes you may think, *"They don't love me. They don't care."* If so, stop right there. Yes, they do. They are just kids. Parents have to prepare for such offenses: "I'm not going to be offended when my kids act like kids. I love them. They don't know what they are doing. And it's okay." The same applies to teenagers and kids reading this—your parents love you. They may not be perfect, but they are loving you the best they know how. Don't let some offense diminish or destroy your relationship with them.

Offenses are certain to occur—even at church. Suppose the devil can get you offended at your pastor, small group leader, or anyone else who attends. The offense will begin to separate you and your family from the very place where God wants to nourish and grow you and your family.

Whether the issue is with a family member, church member, coworker, or even a total stranger, realize your real battle is not against those people. Your spouse, employer, parents, and siblings are not the enemy. If you want to take your frustrations out on somebody, put your energy and efforts into a fight against the spiritual force of wickedness. "For our struggle is not against flesh and blood, but against the rulers, against the authorities, against the powers of this dark world and against the spiritual forces of evil in the heavenly realms" (Ephesians 6:12).

Because we're in a spiritual battle, we must address offenses spiritually. I have found a few guidelines that help me when I start to get offended at someone close to me. These aren't the only things you can do, but will be a good start to help you get unstuck and moving forward:

1. **Believe the best.** Choose to fill in any gaps of information with trust, not suspicion. I have had many instances where I was offended and later realized that the offense was unfounded. I assumed the worst rather than the best.

2. **Give grace.** You never know what's going on in the other person's life or what struggles that person is facing. We judge others by their actions and ourselves by our intentions, but we all need to be more aware of God's great grace.

3. **Pray for the person who has offended you.** It's hard to remain offended at someone you pray for (Ephesians 6:18).

4. **Forgive your offender.** Forgiveness is never easy, but it's always right (Matthew 6:14-15, and review Chapter 2). Below are four steps to help you walk through forgiveness:

   a. Recognize the harm and damage the offense has cost you.

   b. Take action to correct and heal.

   c. Understand what happened and what caused it to happen.

   d. Remember God's forgiveness.

[Again, this is not intended to be an exhaustive explanation. It is a simple resource I learned from my life coach, Randy Powell, to help you get unstuck and move toward becoming unstoppable.]

A Special Word for Men

Emotions are a good thing. Earlier in my life, I never would have considered saying (or writing) such a statement. If you know me personally, you understand. I am not an emotional person, nor do I like to hang out with emotional people. I rarely get overly excited about anything. I like to say I am pretty even-keeled, and I think my wife and kids would agree. Too much emotion makes me uncomfortable.

For example, I don't know what to do when I'm around someone who starts crying. I become awkward in that moment, even as a pastor. But I have learned that part of the reason I lived so much of my life emotionally shut down is because of the pain of disappointment. Remember my story of fishing with Johnny in Chapter 11? It was then that I decided never to get my hopes up or get too excited about what was happening in my life. Living emotionally shut down was a way to protect myself from experiencing any more pain. I can't get hurt if I don't care.

In 2020, I had a moment of clarity. While I was processing my revelation about living shut down emotionally, out of nowhere, I felt God speak to my heart: "If you can't feel pain, you'll never experience My joy." His words deeply touched me. At the time, I had been struggling personally. I was physically tired and emotionally exhausted from the weight of buying our new building added to the usual business of the church . . . and then everything was compounded by the uncertainty of a pandemic. Covid-19 had shut down the country. I just couldn't get motivated to keep moving forward. It was like my gas tank was empty. I started feeling angry and frustrated, and I just wanted to quit.

As all that weight hit me at the same time, I finally realized that the choice I had made as a fifteen-year-old to shut down my emotions to protect my heart was a trap from the enemy. In determining to never get my hopes up again, even if that meant turning off all my emotions, I had short-circuited the very vehicle God designed to give me: His supernatural strength. As long as I refused to experience pain, I was also unable to receive the fullness of God's strength that comes from His joy.

If you refuse to feel pain, you'll never experience joy. And, ultimately, you can't receive God's strength for your life. Nehemiah 8:10 says, "The joy of the Lord is your strength." Emotions are like a see-saw. When one side goes up, the other goes down. However, if neither side goes down, then neither side will go up either. You're stuck. So don't live your life emotionally shut down as I did for so many years. Instead, decide to come alive with God's strength that is available for you to experience through His joy.

Men especially need to hear this message. If you can't experience joy, you'll never have the strength you need, and that's one reason America is full of families where the wife leads the home spiritually. It's because so many husbands are emotionally shut down and limiting themselves spiritually. They lack the strength to lead at the level that God has called them to lead. The enemy has sabotaged men, spiritually weakening them in order to derail and destroy the family unit.

Men, I'm challenging you to allow God to heal every unresolved wound so you can begin to experience the joy of the Lord, which will provide ample strength to make it through all disappointments and defeats. It's time to walk in the power that God has already provided for you.

I want to declare truth over you right now: You are a champion. You are an overcomer (1 John 4:4).

You have power (Luke 24:49; Acts 1:8). You are whole (Colossians 2:10). You might be thinking you're incomplete. No, you are not. When you were born again, wholeness came into your life. You may be thinking you're dysfunctional, just like your dad. Well, God is your heavenly Father now, so it doesn't matter what your earthly father was like. It's time for you to be the man that God has called you to be.

Remember, God Is with You

Sometimes you've got to remind yourself that God's with you. Isaiah 43:2 says, "When you go through deep waters, I will be with you. When you go through rivers of difficulty, you will not drown. When you walk through the fire of oppression, you will not be burned up; the flames will not consume you" (NLT). Regardless of what life throws at you, don't be afraid, for God is with you. God didn't promise us an easy life, but He promised not to abandon us.

I know some of you feel like your world is falling apart. You feel like the house is on fire—maybe not literally, but your "everything" seems to be burning down around you. It reminds me of a story of a young boy whose house caught on fire one night, and he was forced to flee to the roof. His father stood on the ground below with outstretched arms, calling to his son, "Jump! I'll catch you." All the boy could see, however, was flames, smoke, and darkness. As you can imagine, he was afraid. His father yelled again, "Jump! I will catch you." But the boy protested, "Daddy, I can't see you." The father replied, "But I can see you, and that's all that matters, so jump."

I want to assure you that God steps in when you obey. He rarely shows you the whole picture of what He sees, but all you need is for God to tell you what's next. You don't need to figure it all out; you would simply get confused or distracted with all the rest. If you are feeling stuck, just ask God, "What's next?" Then, take the first step . . . and the next step . . . and the next step, and never give up. God's got you. Jump!

Scan here to watch my podcast episode, **"Don't Give Up."**

Next Steps

Although you've reached the end of this book, I assure you it's only the beginning of your journey. I encourage you to go back, reread, and mark the portions that seem to jump out at you. You might want to spend the next twenty-one days focused on just one of the four building blocks of life: identity, purpose, vision, or paradigm, before you move ahead to learn about the others. Trust that God is at work in you and that He will complete the work He's started in your life.

I also want to provide you with some tools and resources for your journey. Scan the QR code to find additional support and material. As you keep being more intentional in your actions, you'll build momentum and begin to live the overcoming, empowered, unstoppable life God designed for you!

Scan the QR code for more
information and free resources.

Index of Chapter Sections

References

1. https://greatergood.berkeley.edu/topic/forgiveness/
   definition#:~:text=Psychologists%20generally%20define%20
   forgiveness%20as,they%20actually%20deserve%20your%20
   forgiveness

2. https://www1.cbn.com/cbnnews/healthscience/2015/june/the-
   deadly-consequences-of-unforgiveness

3. https://www.unite714.com/?locale=en

4. https://www.genesisforordinarypeople.com/faq/why-did-terah-
   leave-the-city-of-ur?c=history-and-genesis

5. C.S. Lewis, *The Screwtape Letters: The Annotated Edition* (Nashville:
   Harper One, 1942, 2013), pp. 167-168

6. https://www.nytimes.com/1983/03/13/travel/footsteps-of-
   abraham-by-malachi-martin.html

   https://www.genesisforordinarypeople.com/faq/why-did-terah-
   leave-the-city-of-ur?c=history-and-genesis

   https://www.thebiblejourney.org/biblejourney2/23-the-journeys-
   of-adam-enoch-noah-abraham/abrams-journey-to-canaan/

7. https://tlexinstitute.com/how-to-effortlessly-have-more-
   positive-thoughts/

8. https://www.forbes.com/sites/margiewarrell/2017/06/15/living-
   on-autopilot-why-your-default-mode-is-derailing-your-
   decisions-and-how-to-stop-it/?sh=60bc97aff0e4

9. https://www.psychologytoday.com/us/basics/identity

10. *Essentialism* by Greg McKeown.

11. "The Human Brain" – https://vimeo.com/54866496

12. https://www.medicinenet.com/what_are_the_3_types_of_
    trauma/article.htm